The STUDENT'S HISTORY
Of NEW MEXICO

The STUDENT'S HISTORY of NEW MEXICO

Facsimile of the Original 1921 Second Edition

by
L. Bradford Prince

New Foreword
and
Suggested Readings
by
Richard Melzer, PhD

SANTA FE

New Material © 2008 by Sunstone Press. All Rights Reserved.

No part of this book may be reproduced in any form or by any electronic or mechanical means including information storage and retrieval systems without permission in writing from the publisher, except by a reviewer who may quote brief passages in a review.

Sunstone books may be purchased for educational, business, or sales promotional use. For information please write: Special Markets Department, Sunstone Press, P.O. Box 2321, Santa Fe, New Mexico 87504-2321.

Library of Congress Cataloging-in-Publication Data

Prince, L. Bradford (Le Baron Bradford), 1840-1922.
  The student's history of New Mexico / by L. Bradford Prince.
    p. cm. -- (Southwest heritage series)
  "Facsimile of the original 1921 second edition with a new foreword and suggested readings by Richard Melzer."
  ISBN 978-0-86534-694-9 (softcover : alk. paper)
  1. New Mexico--History. I. Title.

F796.P83 2009
978.9--dc22
                    2008031207

WWW.SUNSTONEPRESS.COM
SUNSTONE PRESS / POST OFFICE BOX 2321 / SANTA FE, NM 87504-2321 /USA
(505) 988-4418 / ORDERS ONLY (800) 243-5644 / FAX (505) 988-1025

The Southwest Heritage Series is dedicated to Jody Ellis and Marcia Muth Miller, the founders of Sunstone Press, whose original purpose and vision continues to inspire and motivate our publications.

CONTENTS

THE SOUTHWEST HERITAGE SERIES / I

FOREWORD TO THIS EDITION / II

FACSIMILE OF 1921 SECOND EDITION / III

I

THE SOUTHWEST HERITAGE SERIES

The history of the United States is written in hundreds of regional histories and literary works. Those letters, essays, memoirs, biographies and even collections of fiction are often first-hand accounts by people who wanted to memorialize an event, a person or simply record for posterity the concerns and issues of the times. Many of these accounts have been lost, destroyed or overlooked. Some are in private or public collections but deemed to be in too fragile condition to permit handling by contemporary readers and researchers.

However, now with the application of twenty-first century technology, nineteenth and twentieth century material can be reprinted and made accessible to the general public. These early writings are the DNA of our history and culture and are essential to understanding the present in terms of the past.

The Southwest Heritage Series is a form of literary preservation. Heritage by definition implies legacy and these early works are our legacy from those who have gone before us. To properly present and preserve that legacy, no changes in style or contents have been made. The material reprinted stands on its own as it first appeared. The point of view is that of the author and the era in which he or she lived. We would not expect photographs of people from the past to be re-imaged with modern clothes, hair styles and backgrounds. We should not, therefore, expect their ideas and personal philosophies to reflect our modern concepts.

Remember, reading their words and sharing their thoughts is a passport back into understanding how the past was shaped and how it influenced today's world.

Our hope is that new access to these older books will provide readers with a challenging and exciting experience.

II

FOREWORD TO THIS EDITION
with
Suggested Readings
by
Richard Melzer, PhD

LeBaron Bradford Prince (1840–1922) was a transplanted New Yorker, a tireless judge, a controversial territorial governor, a gentleman scholar, and an early leader of the Historical Society of New Mexico. In all these roles, and others, he was a passionate advocate of New Mexico statehood. In the words of Robert W. Larson, the foremost authority on the struggle for New Mexico statehood, Prince displayed a readiness "to plunge into the statehood fray" whenever and wherever he was needed.

Prince was born, raised, and educated in New York. As a young attorney, his political career in state politics had progressed well until he clashed with leaders of the state Republican Party machine, led by Roscoe Conkling. Salvaging his political fortunes in the West, Prince won appointment as the chief justice of the New Mexico Supreme Court in 1879. By all accounts, no territorial judge worked harder than Prince, often hearing cases from 8:00 in the morning till 11:00 at night. In what time remained in his busy days, Prince compiled a 603-page volume of territorial laws and began to write history with the clear purpose of advocating New Mexico statehood. His first work on New Mexico history, entitled *Historical Sketches of New Mexico: From the Earliest Records to the American Occupation*, appeared in 1883.

After actively lobbying for the coveted position, Prince won appointment as the thirteenth U.S. territorial governor of New Mexico. Unfortunately, his four-year term in office, 1889–93, was marred by property violence (by the *Gorras Blancas*), political violence (by and against the Santa Fe Ring), and almost continuous political controversy.

Despite this turmoil, Prince and his wife Mary were known for their generous hospitality at the Palace of the Governors, sparing little to entertain visitors of all social classes.

In relation to his overriding political goal, Prince convened a state constitutional convention shortly after he entered the governor's office. Knowing that the writing of a state constitution was a major step toward statehood, the governor praised the convention's work as "excellent" but blamed his uncompromising Democratic opponents for the draft's decisive defeat at the polls. In 1890 Prince led a delegation of twenty-nine territorial leaders on a trip to Washington, D.C., to lobby for statehood, among other pressing issues. Unfortunately, the sojourn east proved as futile as the drive to pass an acceptable state constitution.

Once out of office, Prince continued to press for New Mexico statehood, especially through the preservation of the region's long history. Realizing that those outside New Mexico thought of the territory's racial diversity as a disadvantage, Prince argued that each racial group (or at least its leaders) had special qualities that had helped to unite, rather than divide the territory during most of its history. Writing to the editor of the *New York Tribune*, Prince asserted that the sum of these special qualities gave New Mexico "special advantages as a self-governing community over most other Territories" that seemed destined to achieve statehood before New Mexico. These "special advantages" became the major theme of Prince's historical work, whether he was collecting artifacts for the Historical Society of New Mexico, serving as that organization's president and most active member from 1884 to World War I, speaking to civic groups, or writing pertinent history, including *New Mexico's Struggle for Statehood*, published in 1910.

L. Bradford Prince was one of seven territorial governors who attended the January 15th inauguration of New Mexico's first state governor, William C. McDonald, in New Mexico's long-awaited statehood year, 1912. Within a year of that auspicious occasion, Prince published *A Concise History of New Mexico*, a condensation and revision of his *Historical Sketches* of 1883. His purpose in 1913 was to be concise by avoiding the "temptation" to provide excessive historical details, a mild criticism of much longer recent histories by Ralph Emerson Twitchell (five volumes, 1911–17) and Benjamin Read (1912). Prince also hoped that his "little volume" might be of use in the now-required teaching of New Mexico history in the state's public schools. The passage of a public school bill during his term as governor had been considered an important step toward the attainment of statehood. The publication of a state history textbook was meant to be an important contribution to New Mexico public education once statehood had been achieved.

But within a year of its publication, Prince affirmed that the length and price of the already brief *Concise History* was excessive for most public schools and students. While still recommending *A Concise History* for teachers and most adults, Prince offered an even more focused, 174-page work, entitled *The Student's History of New Mexico*.

Now, instead of using history to argue the case for New Mexico statehood, Prince's chief goal was to use history to help create pride in New Mexico for the "clear-eyed, pure hearted, noble minded youth" of the nation's newest state. These future citizens could take pride in both their past, "the most interesting of all American state histories," and in the special qualities of individual groups whose collective story was "unrivaled in ancient or modern times." Proud students would hopefully grow to become good citizens, well prepared to contribute to the making of a strong, modern state. Convinced that *The Student's History* had served its purpose well, Prince later updated his book with an additional ten pages about New Mexico's first few years of statehood. This second edition of *The Student's History* appeared in 1921, a year before Prince's death.

Despite its brevity, *The Student's History* reflects much about Prince and his Anglo generation's thinking about New Mexico and its past, as of the early twentieth century. By our twenty-first century standards, much of this thinking is imperialistic, elitist, and racist. While Prince described most Spanish, Anglo, and Pueblo leaders in appreciative terms and portrayed four of New Mexico's "most noted" Indian fighters with special praise, readers search in vain for references to Navajo or Apache leaders like Geronimo or Cochise, no less for any virtues these Native Americans may have displayed for students to admire and emulate.

The second edition of *The Student's History* is also offered as a brief history of New Mexico of value to the general reader sophisticated enough to recognize its biases, but astute enough to appreciate its many facts. If this unique telling of New Mexico's past adds to our pride in being New Mexicans—or helps others to better understand New Mexico—then L. Bradford Prince will have achieved his purpose long after he departed his beloved New Mexico, once a striving territory and now a productive member of the nation's family of states.

SUGGESTED READINGS

Clancey, Frank W. *In Memory of L. Bradford Prince.* Santa Fe: Historical Society of New Mexico, 1923.

Donlon, Walter J. "LeBaron Bradford Prince, Chief Justice and Governor of New Mexico Territory, 1879–1893." Unpublished Ph.D. dissertation, University of New Mexico, 1967.

Lamar, Howard R. *The Far Southwest, 1846–1912: A Territorial History.* Albuquerque: University of New Mexico Press, 2000.

Larson, Robert W. *New Mexico's Quest for Statehood, 1846–1912.* Albuquerque: University of New Mexico Press, 1968.

Montoya, María E. "L. Bradford Prince: The Education of a Gilded Age Politician." *New Mexico Historical Review*, vol. 66 (April 1991): 179–201.

Pattison, J. Michael. "Four 'Gentlemen' Historians of New Mexico." Unpublished M.A. thesis, New Mexico Highlands University, 1992.

Poldervaart, Arie W. *Black-Robed Justice: A History of the Administration of Justice in New Mexico from the American Occupation in 1846 Until Statehood in 1912.* Santa Fe: Historical Society of New Mexico, 1948.

Stensvaag, James T. "Cleo On the Frontier: The Intellectual Evolution of the Historical Society of New Mexico, 1859–1925." *New Mexico Historical Review*, vol. 55 (October 1980): 293–308.

COLLECTED PAPERS

L. Bradford Prince Papers, Center for Southwest Research, Zimmerman Library, University of New Mexico, Albuquerque, New Mexico.

L. Bradford Prince Papers, New Mexico State Records Center and Archives, Santa Fe, New Mexico.

MAIN HISTORICAL WORKS BY L. BRADFORD PRINCE

Prince, L. Bradford. *A Concise History of New Mexico*. Cedar Rapids, Iowa: The Torch Press, 1912.

_____. *Historical Sketches of New Mexico: From the Earliest Records to the American Occupation*. New York: Leggat Brothers, 1883.

_____. *New Mexico's Struggle for Statehood: Sixty Years of Effort to Obtain Self Government*. Santa Fe: New Mexico Printing Company, 1910.

_____. *Spanish Mission Churches of New Mexico*. Santa Fe: Museum of New Mexico Press, 1976; originally published in 1915.

_____. *The Student's History of New Mexico*. Denver: The Publishers Press, 1913; second edition, 1921.

III

FACSIMILE OF 1921 SECOND EDITION

The Student's History of New Mexico

BY

L. BRADFORD PRINCE, LL. D.

President of the Historical Society of New Mexico; Vice-Pres. of the National Historical Society; Hon. Member of the American Numismatic and Archæological Society; Hon. Member of the Missouri Historical Society; of the Kansas Historical Society; of the Wisconsin Historical Society; Cor. Member of the Texas Historical Society; of the Minnesota Historical Society, Etc. Etc.

SECOND EDITION
WITH SUPPLEMENT TO 1921

THE PUBLISHERS PRESS
DENVER, COLORADO
1921

Copyright, 1913, by
L. Bradford Prince

The Governor's Palace, Santa Fe.

Contents

	PAGE
PREFACE	9

CHAPTER I
NEW MEXICO IN GENERAL 11
NAME 11
BOUNDARIES 12
CAPITAL 13
POPULATION 14

CHAPTER II
THE ABORIGINES 16

CHAPTER III
THE PUEBLO INDIANS 20

CHAPTER IV
CABEZA DE VACA 32

CHAPTER V
FRIAR MARCOS DE NIZA 37

CHAPTER VI
CORONADO 41

CHAPTER VII
FRIAR RUIZ AND ESPEJO 50

CHAPTER VIII
ATTEMPTS AT COLONIZATION—1585-1598 . . 55
CASTANO DE SOSA 55
BONILLA AND HUMANA 57

CHAPTER IX
THE CONQUEST BY ONATE 59

CHAPTER X
SPANISH OCCUPATION—1598-1680 65

CHAPTER XI
THE PUEBLO REVOLUTION 73

CONTENTS.

	PAGE
CHAPTER XII THE RE-CONQUEST	77
CHAPTER XIII THE SPANISH ERA—1696-1822	81
CHAPTER XIV THE EXPEDITION OF LIEUTENANT PIKE—1806	88
CHAPTER XV MEXICAN GOVERNMENT—1821-1846	95
PIONEERS	99
TEXAN SANTA FE EXPEDITION	99
CHAPTER XVI THE INSURRECTION OF 1837	103
CHAPTER XVII THE SANTA FE TRAIL	106
CHAPTER XVIII SPANISH AND MEXICAN GOVERNORS	113
CHAPTER XIX THE AMERICAN OCCUPATION	116
CHAPTER XX U. S. PROVISIONAL GOVERNMENT—1846-1851	122
CHAPTER XXI THE TERRITORIAL PERIOD—1851-1912	125
CHAPTER XXII CHURCHES	157
SCHOOLS	164
NEWSPAPERS	167
CHAPTER XXIII TERRITORIAL OFFICIALS	170
CHAPTER XXIV STATE ORGANIZATION, 1912	173

List of Illustrations

	PAGE
GOVERNOR'S PALACE, SANTA FE	Frontispiece
MOQUI INDIAN DANCE	18
ANCIENT STONE IDOLS	21
ESTUFA IN SANTO DOMINGO	24
COCHITI PUEBLO; FAVORITE GUIDE	26
ISLETA WOMAN AND CHILD	30
ANCIENT TURQUOISE MINE	35
OLD CHURCH AT SAN JUAN	66
SAN JUAN PUEBLO, FESTIVAL	68
RUINS OF PECOS CHURCH	69
INTERIOR OF PECOS CHURCH	71
CHURCH OF SAN MIGUEL	79
PENUELA AUTOGRAPH	82
GENERAL ARMIJO	97
STREET IN SANTA FE, 1880	111
GEN. JOSE MARIA CHAVEZ	126
COL. MANUEL CHAVES	127
HON. ROMAN A. BACA	128
KIT CARSON	129
GENERAL LEW WALLACE	140
BEN HUR ROOM IN PALACE	142
FIRST CAPITOL AFTER FIRE	146
NEW CAPITOL	150
FOUR GOVERNORS	151
SIGNING THE ENABLING ACT	154
DOOR OF SANTO DOMINGO CHURCH	158
ARCHBISHOP LAMY	160
THE BISHOP'S GARDEN	161

Preface

THE History of New Mexico is the most interesting of all American State Histories. It presents a greater variety than any other, and tells of three distinct nationalities, as different in their characteristics as can well be—the Pueblo Indian, the Spanish and the American.

It is as full of romance as any tale of the Middle Ages. The remarkable journey of Cabeza de Vaca; the brilliant expedition of Coronado; the touching story of the missionary zeal of Friar Ruiz; the gallant attempt at rescue by Espejo; the epic poem of Villagrá describing the colonization by Oñate; the wonderful capture of Acoma by Saldivar; the rapid re-conquest under De Vargas; the long years of patient suffering from Indian invasion and depredation; the thrilling stories of the Santa Fé Trail; the unequaled march of Kearny across the Plains; the long Struggle for Statehood; the marvelous progress in development and education; all of these unite to make a story unrivaled in ancient or modern times.

It is this wonderful record of exploration and discovery, of chivalry and heroism, of sacrifice and devotion, of suffering and endurance, of marches and battles, of energy and ambition, of enterprise and achievement, which is briefly presented in this volume.

It is dedicated to the clear-eyed, pure hearted, noble minded youth of New Mexico, who are the hope of its future.

When it was first suggested that a history of less size and price than the "Concise History of New Mexico" should be written for the use of schools, etc., the first idea was to put it in a more familiar if not story-like form and to change the arrangement of several subjects. But a little thought made it obvious that it would be to the advantage of both teacher and scholar, to follow the Concise History in the arrangement of chapters and subjects, so that if the teacher has a copy of that book he or she can supplement the facts stated in the Student's History by others connected with or illustrating them, mentioned in the corresponding chapter of the larger work, and thus the scholar will have the benefit of everything contained in the latter. Much of this volume therefore is a condensation or abridgment of the Concise History, preserving the arrangement of subjects with but little change.

The illustrations, with few exceptions, have been made expressly for this book and in several cases are from photographs believed to be unique.

CHAPTER I.

Name, Boundaries, Population, Capital.

NAME

The oldest state name in the United States is that of New Mexico, with the single exception of Florida.

The latter, as is well-known, was given to the peninsula by Ponce de Leon on his discovery of its shores in 1512; some consider it was so named on account of the discovery being made on Easter Day, called by the Spaniards "Pascua Florida;" and others, that it was to designate it as the "Land of Flowers."

The name of New Mexico first appears in the narrative of Antonio de Espejo, in 1583, having been given to the fifteen provinces which he discovered on his expedition, as we are told by the historian Gonzales de Mendoza, "because it is similar in many things to the other Mexico already discovered." The narrative of Espejo's exploration was published in Madrid in 1586, the description of the newly found region was soon known to all the world, and the name, New Mexico, immediately received the ratification of universal adoption.

At different times before the attainment of statehood, attempts were made to change the name, and Lincoln, Montezuma, Acoma, etc., were among the names proposed; but no success attended the efforts, and the new state was admitted under the old historic name it had borne for over three centuries.

Pet Name

As nearly all of the older states have pet names, such as the "Empire State" for New York, the "Bay State" for Massachusetts, the "Granite State" for New Hampshire, etc., so New Mexico is called the "Sunshine State".

This originated in the fall of 1891, when the editor of King's Handbook wrote to Gov. L. B. Prince inquiring for the pet name to be inserted in the article on New Mexico in the Handbook. Governor Prince answered that none had been regularly adopted, but suggested that "Sunshine State" would be most appropriate.

This was published, and the name received universal approval and acceptance at home and abroad. In 1893, at the Chicago Exposition, September 16th was celebrated as New Mexico Day, and one of the principal features was the recitation by Capt. Jack Crawford of an original poem entitled "The Sunshine State", which concluded as follows:

"Soon will thy plains and lofty mountains teem
  With men whose tireless hands will shape thy fate,
And on the roster of the earth, supreme,
  Engrave thy honored name, O! Sunshine State."

More recently Dr. Gray, President of the University, wrote "The Song of the Sunshine State", which ends with these lines:

"O! Queen of our devotion,
  To thee we dedicate
Our loving hearts, New Mexico,
  Thou blessed Sunshine State."

BOUNDARIES

The boundaries of New Mexico, from the first, were very indefinite. On the west it reached to the South Sea, as the Pacific Ocean was then called, and on the north there was no claimant to prevent its extension to the Arctic regions. On the south, it began where the northern provinces of Mexico—New Galicia and New Biscay—ended, but with no established boundary; and on the east, for over a century, it divided the country with Florida, which occupied all the region commencing at the Atlantic and extending westward beyond the Mississippi.

After settlements were made along the Mississippi, and the valley of that river became known as Louisiana, there were three divisions in the midst of the continent, instead of two, Louisiana coming between Florida and New Mexico; and after another interval, the Pacific coast separated itself and was distinguished as California.

After the independence of Mexico, by the treaty of January 12, 1828, between that country and the United States, the hundredth degree of longitude became the eastern boundary of New Mexico, and the Nepesta or Arkansas River its limit on the north.

Texas, when it declared its independence, claimed to own all the territory east of the Rio Grande; a claim which was absurd when it is remembered that it would have taken Santa Fe, which during almost two and a half centuries had been the capital of New Mexico, out of the country of which it was the political center.

By the treaty of Guadalupe Hidalgo, all of New Mexico was ceded to the United States. While its southern boundary was definitely fixed by the treaty, in other directions its extent was left indefinite; and this condition continued until the organization by Congress of the Territory of New Mexico, by the Act of September 9, 1850.

At the same time, the northwesterly portion of what had before been New Mexico was made into the Territory of Utah.

On December 30, 1853, the Gadsden Purchase treaty was signed, by which the United States bought from Mexico a long strip of territory, extending from the Rio Grande to the Gila, for ten million dollars; and by Act of Congress of August 4, 1854, this was added to New Mexico.

In 1863, Congress established the Territory of Arizona, consisting of all of New Mexico west of the 109th meridian, and on December 29th of that year, the new territory was officially organized at Navajo Springs.

This reduced the area of New Mexico almost one-half, and it was further curtailed a few years later, when by the Act of Congress of March 2, 1867, all that portion of the territory north of the 37th parallel of latitude was attached to Colorado. This left it as it still exists, with an average width of 335 miles, a length on its eastern boundary of 345 miles, and on the western boundary of 390; and with a total area of 121,469 square miles.

CAPITAL

For fully three centuries the city of Santa Fe has been the capital of New Mexico. For seven years after the first colonization, from 1598-1605, the seat of the new government was at San Gabriel, at the junction of the Rio Grande and the Chama; but it was then removed to Santa Fe, where it has ever since remained.

Among all the capitals of the United States, Santa Fe stands unique. For antiquity it is the acknowledged head, counting many more years than Boston, which is its nearest rival. It is not only the oldest capital in the United States, but with one exception the oldest in all America; and it antedates by many years the capitals of the two most powerful empires of continental Europe, Germany and Russia.

POPULATION

In the population of New Mexico, the increase for a long time was very slow.

By a census of 1760, the Spanish population was 7,666, and the Pueblo Indian 9,104.

In 1793, the Spaniards had increased to 16,156 and the Indians were returned at 9,275.

Governor Chacon made an official report in 1799, showing a white population of 18,826, together with 9,732 Pueblo Indians.

Another census was taken in 1805, the report of which was made by Governor Alencaster, containing the following figures: Spaniards—male 10,390, female 10,236, total 20,626; Pueblo Indians—male 4,094, female 4,078, total 8,182; grand total of population of 28,798. In all of these cases the wild tribes of Indians are excluded. The report of Governor Melgares in 1820 gives the Spanish population at 28,436. In 1821, Father Rubi states the number of Pueblo Indians to be 9,034.

The census reports under the Republic of Mexico made no distinction of race, so that only the aggregate can be given: being 43,433 in 1827, as reported by Narbona; and 55,403 in 1840, as reported by Governor Armijo.

Since the American occupation, the decennial census reports give the following figures, showing a steady and fairly rapid increase:

1850 61,547
1860 80,567
1870 91,874
1880 119,565
1890 153,593
1900 195,310
1910 327,301

The population by the last census, in 1910, is divided among the counties as follows:

Bernalillo	23,606
Chaves	16,850
Colfax	16,460
Curry	11,443
Doña Ana	12,893
Eddy	12,400
Grant	14,813
Guadalupe	10,927
Lincoln	7,822
Luna	3,913
McKinley	12,963
Mora	12,611
Otero	7,069
Quay	14,912
Rio Arriba	16,624
Roosevelt	12,064
San Juan	8,504
San Miguel	22,930
Sandoval	8,579
Santa Fe	14,770
Sierra	3,536
Socorro	14,761
Taos	12,008
Torrance	10,119
Union	11,404
Valencia	13,320

CHAPTER II.

The Aborigines

New Mexico's history naturally falls into three great divisions, representing not only distinct epochs, but different nationalities —the Aboriginal and Pueblo, the Spanish and Mexican, and the American.

While these are absolutely distinct, yet all three epochs are still represented by existing villages and people; so the observer may in a single day visit an Indian pueblo exhibiting the customs of the intelligent natives of three and a half centuries ago; a Mexican town, where the architecture, the language and the habits of the people are those which were brought from Spain in the days of Cortez, and Coronado; and an American community, full of the characteristics of modern western life.

Before taking up the thread of written history, which begins with the arrival of the first Europeans, we must briefly consider the people who, for long centuries before, had inhabited the country, and whose descendants still form one of the most interesting portions of its population.

New Mexico was far from being a new or unknown land when it was first seen by Spanish eyes. On the contrary, if the figures given by the narrators are to be taken as correct, it contained more people than it does now, and whether this was true or not, the vast number of ruins which are wide-spread over the territory, is evidence that at some period of the olden time a great multitude of human beings found their homes, and passed their lives, in the valleys and on the mesas of what is now New Mexico.

Unfortunately for the historian, they possessed no written language, and no system of hieroglyphics to perpetuate the record of events. In an interesting speech made by the governor of the Pueblo of Zuñi, in Santa Fe, on the first day of the great "Tertio-Millennial" historical pageant of 1883, his opening words were very significant, in this connection. He said: "The Great Spirit has given to his children of different races various gifts; all of great value, but each diverse from the other. To his white children he has given the great gift of handing down knowledge from one generation to another by the means of marks or letters. To his red children he did not give this good gift. But he gave them another in its place. Of his fatherly affection he gave them Great Memories, of unfailing power; so that the story of the past, handed down from old to young, is transmitted, unchanged, from generation to generation."

There can be no doubt that a vast amount of legendary lore is thus orally transmitted; being taught with utmost care, and jealously guarded from accidental change or the chance of loss through death, by being held by three men—a kind of three-fold chain—who communicate it, word for word, to their successors.

If the matter thus carefully repeated was mainly historic, we might have a good substitute for the written book; but it is mostly mythological and ceremonial, and far too fanciful for prosaic historical use.

For the few facts that can be learned, therefore, of conditions that existed before the coming of the Spaniards, we have to depend most largely on the records preserved among the more cultivated people to the south, in the land of Montezuma.

The people found by Cortez in the land then called Anahuac, and which is now the Republic of Mexico, had come thither by a succession of migrations, all of which were from the north and northwest.

The first of these, of which there is any distinct knowledge, was that of the Toltecs. They are said to have left their original home in the far northwest, in the year 1 Tecpatl. They traveled leisurely, remaining sometimes for years in a locality which suited their fancy and then marching rapidly forward, until another favored spot attracted their attention. Thus they proceeded for somewhat over a century, until they arrived at a place in the great valley of Mexico, which they called Tollantzinco, and there they established their capital.

Both Clavigero and Gondra, who are acknowledged authorities, fix the date of the arrival of the Toltecs in Anahuac, as the year 648. For five centuries they controlled the land of their adoption, and they are believed to have been the architects of the great structures, the ruins of which still exist in central and southern Mexico. Then, for reasons now impossible to ascertain, they disappeared towards the south.

The next migration was that of the Chichimecas, a rough and uncivilized people, who also came from the same direction in the north. They had heard of the land of plenty in the south, and marched under Xolotl, the brother of their king, in search of

Moqui Indian Dance.

its luxuriance and riches. Torquemada says that they originally lived in caves in the mountains, which tradition may be connected with the most ancient of the cliff and cave dwellings, whose remains still exist. The date of their arrival in Mexico is fixed by Clavigero at the year 1170.

They were soon followed, only thirty years after, by the

Acolhuans, an intelligent and ingenious people, who established themselves at Tescuco, on the eastern border of the great Mexican lake, where they were found by the Spaniards when Cortez arrived.

About the same time, came the end of the long migration of the Aztecs, who settled not far from the last preceding comers.

According to the prevailing legend, they were to continue to journey until they should see an eagle perched upon a cactus, holding a snake in its mouth; and this sign, according to the story, was found near Chapultepec; and the place thus providentially designated was instantly recognized, and established as their future capital.

Most of the authorities trace the route of their pilgrimage as passing through Arizona, so as to make the Casa Grande one of its places of sojourn; but others think that their course was more easterly, and that many of the most remarkable ruins in New Mexico are the results of their residence there. There can be little or no doubt that the people whom Coronado and Espejo, found at Zuñi and Moqui, and in the Rio Grande Valley, living in substantial houses several stories in height, cultivating the fields, raising cotton and corn, enjoying an excellent form of government, and in all respects entirely different from the wild and nomadic tribes of the plains who surrounded them, were the remains of one or another of these great migrations.

CHAPTER III.

The Pueblo Indians

We come now to the native people of New Mexico as they have existed in historic times. The earliest views we have of them are not continuous, but rather like the glimpses of a landscape by flashes of lightning in the darkness of the night. We have a momentary view as Marcos de Niza saw from afar the terraced houses of Cibola, in 1539. Two years pass, and the historians of Coronado's expedition give us the first intelligent account of the people as they appeared in 1541-42. Then over a generation passes by before we have another glimpse, in the record from the pen of Espejo. That was in 1583; and then again there is silence until Oñate comes with permanent colonization in 1598.

In the time of Coronado's expedition, according to the list given by Castañeda, he had knowledge of seventy-one towns or pueblos, which he designates as follows: Cibola, 7; Tusayan, 7; Acuco, 1; Tihuex, 12; Tutahaco, 8; Quirix, 7; Snowy Mountains, 7; Ximena, 3; Cicuyc, 1; Jemez, 7; Aguas Calientes, 3; Yuqueyunque, 6; Valladolid, called Braba, 1; Chia, 1.

Espejo, in his description of the country, forty years afterward, reports about the same number, though somewhat differently arranged. His list contains the following: On the Rio Grande below Albuquerque, 10; Tihuas, 16; province east of Rio Grande, 11; Quires, 5; Cunames (Zia, etc.), 5; Amies or Amejes (Jemez), 7; Acoma, 1; Cibola, 6; Hubates, 5; Tamos, 3; besides some referred to but without exact names or numbers.

Today there exist but 19 in all, 18 in the Valley of the Rio Grande and its tributaries, and one at Zuñi; thus showing a great diminution in number since the advent of the Europeans. This can be accounted for in various ways. In the first place it was the policy of the Spanish government, to consolidate the Indian population in a comparatively small number of villages or pueblos, for various reasons, both political and religious. Then came the revolution of 1680, and the extraordinary reduction in the Indian numbers during the brief period of their

Ancient Stone Idols.
(From Historical Society Collection.)

control. Almost constant wars resulted in the destruction or abandonment of many of the pueblos. We have an exact list made shortly after the re-conquest of the country, and it differs very little from that of today. An official list, made by Governor Mendoza in 1742, gives the names as follows, exclusive of the Moquis:

"Taos, Picuries, San Juan, San Ildefonso, Santa Clara, Pojuaque, Nambe, and Tesuque, north of Santa Fe; Pecos east, and Galisteo south of Santa Fe; Cochiti, Santo Domingo, San Felipe, Santa Ana, Zia, Jemez, Laguna, Acoma, Zuni, and Isleta, south or west of Santa Fe."

In 1805, Governor Alencaster caused a complete census to be made of the province, which resulted in showing a Spanish population of 26,805, and 8,172 Pueblo Indians. As this is probably accurate and contains the mission names of the respective pueblos, it is inserted in full, as follows:

San Geronimo de Taos	508
San Lorenzo de Picuries	250
San Juan de los Caballeros	194
Santo Tomas de Abiquiu	134
Santa Clara	186
San Ildefonso	175
San Francisco de Nambé	143
N. S. de Guadalupe de Pojuaque	100
San Diego de Tesuque	131
N. S. de los Angeles de Pecos	104
San Buena Ventura de Cochití	656
Santo Domingo	333
San Felipe	289
N. S. de los Dolores de Sandia	314
San Diego de Jemez	264
N. S. de la Asumpcion de Zia	254
Santa Ana	450
San Agustin del Isleta	419
N. S. de Belen	107
San Estevan de Acoma	731
San Josef de La Laguna	940
N. S. de Guadalupe de Zuñi	1470

From the names of the patron saints to whom the Indian towns were dedicated can also be ascertained the festival day of each of the pueblos mentioned.

THE PUEBLO INDIANS. 23

The only changes which have taken place in the hundred years since Governor Alencaster's census have been in the dropping of Abiquiu and Belen as distinct pueblos, and in the abandonment of the pueblo of Pecos, in the year 1840, and the removal of its surviving inhabitants to Jemez.

The latest available statistics give the population as stated below, which shows that while there are considerable gains or losses in particular pueblos, yet, in the aggregate, the Indian population has continued almost the same during the past century.

Taos 533
Picuris 126
San Juan 376
Santa Clara 264
San Ildefonso 115
Nambé 112
Pojuaque 16
Tesuque 95
Cochití 234
Santo Domingo 872
San Felipe 517
Sandia 76
Jemez 555
Zia 118
Santa Ana 221
Isleta 1057
Acoma 857
Laguna 1616
Zuñi 1525

9285

The grants of land to the different Pueblo communities were made after the revolution of 1680, and while the Spaniards were still at El Paso, awaiting the re-conquest of the province. This action seems to have been taken as a measure of conciliation by Governor Cruzate, in view of his contemplated re-entrance into New Mexico.

As a rule the grants are squares, containing about 17,360

acres, the sides being a Spanish league distant in each direction from the church in the center of the pueblo.

These grants have all since been confirmed by the government of the United States, so that each pueblo has an absolute title to its land.

Estufa in Santo Domingo.

Turning now to the customs and manner of life of the Pueblo Indians, we have descriptions from Castañeda and Espejo, and many particulars in the Epic of Villagrá, and from other records of the early occupations; and all of these agree as well as can be expected of observations made by men of different tastes and temperaments, who are describing matters that are novel to them.

Castañeda gives us quite full descriptions of the towns and people of Cibola, Tihuex, and Cicuic, the substance of which may be summed up as follows:

"The towns are built in a square, around a plaza in the center, in which are the estufas. The houses are four stories high; the roofs arranged in terraces, all the same height, so that the people can make a tour of the whole town without having to cross a single street. The houses have no doors below, but are entered by movable ladders, which reach to the balconies on the inside of the square.

"The houses are built in common. The women mix the mortar and build the walls. The men bring the wood and construct the frames.

"The young men who are not yet married serve the public in general. They live in the estufas, which are under-ground in the plazas of the town; and of which some are square and some are round. The roofs of the estufas are supported by pillars made of the trunks of pine trees. In the center is a fire-place, with a fire burning therein, on which they throw from time to time a handful of sage, which suffices to keep up the heat. The roof is on a level with the ground. When a young man marries, it is by order of the aged men who govern. He has to spin and weave a mantle; they then bring the young girl to him; he covers her shoulders with it and she becomes his wife.

The houses are well arranged and kept in good order; one room is devoted to cooking and another to grinding grain. The latter contains a fire-place and three stones set in masonry; three women sit down before the stones; the first breaks the grain, the second crushes it, and the third grinds it entirely to powder. In all the province glazed pottery abounds and the earthen jars or vessels are of curious and beautiful form and workmanship."

Espejo tells us that the people wore clothing of cotton and of deer skin, and shoes, with soles made of the strongest and best leather. They raised great quantities of cotton, from which many of their garments were made; and the beautiful and curious mantles, especially at Zia, were equal to anything of European manufacture. He also speaks of the houses in Zia, being the most beautiful the Spaniards had seen among similar native

Cochiti' Pueblo, Favorite Guide.

races, well-plastered, and painted in many colors. He makes special mention of the idols or household gods of the people, which he found in all of the localities he visited.

His attention was attracted by the great amount of food stored up to be used in time of need, and the "infinity of hens" found in various parts of the country. Referring to their arms, he says that they had very strong bows, and arrows with points of flint, with which they were able to pierce a coat of mail, and he speaks of the macanas—the characteristic weapons of the Pueblo Indians—as being half a yard in length and covered with sharp points of flint, with which they could with ease cut a man in two.

The descriptions of Benavides, written nearly half a century later, in 1526, are valuable and interesting, as they are the result of long experience among the people after the Spanish occupation.

As to the success of agriculture his language is scarcely less enthusiastic than that of Castañeda.

In those days the streams were full of fish, of which he enumerates no less than eight varieties, and the plains and forests abounded in game.

He speaks of the curious division of labor which seems to have been characteristic of the Pueblos at all times. "Among these nations, the custom is for the women to build the walls of the houses, while the men spin and weave, and go to war and the chase," referring to this fact in connection with the large number of churches that had been erected, "which have been built entirely by the women and the boys and girls."

As to dress, he says, "all the people are clothed in mantas of cotton or of skin; and they wear ornaments as far as they are able; particularly necklaces and earrings of turquoise."

In almost all respects these descriptions, written by the earliest observers, agree with the habits and customs of the Pueblo Indians of today. Few races have been more changeless in such matters. The modifications most noticeable are the results of altered conditions which rendered the old system obsolete.

The wonderfully business-like way in which all the public business of the town is conducted, and the readiness with which the entire energy and force of the community can be directed in a moment to any work of general public concern, are matters of surprise and admiration to those not accustomed to them.

Some mention must be made of the peculiarity of their languages, and of the distinction which exists between the various groups of pueblos and gives rise to that peculiarity.

The Pueblo Indians were distinctly divided into several great families, or "nations," as the older writers call them. The term "Pueblo" Indian is comparatively modern, being used to designate all of the "town" Indians as distinguished from the wild tribes who had no permanent villages; but in the earlier records the particular "nacion" is always mentioned. The leading groups of nations were the Tehuas, Queres, Tanos, Tihuas, Piros, and Tompiros. Several of the groups of the greatest importance at the time of the Spanish occupation were practically destroyed during the twelve years of the Revolution, or have gradually dwindled into unimportance. Among these are the Piros, Tanos, and Tompiros.

One of the most careful descriptions that we have of the different nations is that of Padre Alonzo de Benavides, above referred to, who made a very full and interesting report of the condition of the country and people in 1626. He described the various divisions of the Pueblo Indians as follows:

"1. PIROS.

"On the Rio Grande, with Senecu, Socorro and Sevilleta as their principal points.

"2. TIHUAS.

"With fifteen or sixteen pueblos and seven thousand people.

"3. QUERES.

"With seven pueblos, of which San Felipe was the first.

"4. TOMPIROS.

"East of the river, with fourteen or fifteen pueblos, and eleven thousand souls. This nation had Abó and Tabira as two of its principal towns.

"5. TANOS.

"North of the Tompiros, having five pueblos with 4,000 inhabitants. These were the Galisteo towns, including San Marcos, San Lazaro, etc.

"6. PECOS.

"The Indians of Pecos belonged to the Jemez nation, but being situated alone, are considered separately, though they speak the Jemez language

"7. TEHUAS.
"Westward again, towards the Rio Grande, are the TEHUAS, with eight pueblos and 6,000 persons.
"8. JEMEZ.
"Though half depopulated by famine and war, yet it contained 3,000 people.
"9. PICURIS.
"With 2,000 inhabitants. It belongs to the Tihua family but is disconnected and distant.
"10. TAOS.
"With 2,500 people. Of the same national stock as Picuris, but with a slight variation of language.
"11. ACOMA, on its 'Peñol,' with about 2,000 souls.
"12. ZUNI.
"With 11 or 12 pueblos, and 10,000 inhabitants."

Coming down to recent times the groups are much simplified. Of the Piros and Tompiros none remain.

Of the Tihuas, in the region where they were so numerous in the time of Coronado, only Isleta and Sandia still exist; with Taos and Picuris in the north.

Of the Queres, we have Santa Ana, Zia, San Felipe, Cochití, Santo Domingo, Laguna and Acoma.

Of the Tehuas, we have San Juan, Santa Clara, Nambé, San Ildefonso, Pojuaque, and Tesuque.

Jemez, including the Pecos Indians, has some similarity to the Tanos; but the two pueblos of Jemez and Pecos are rather to be considered as forming a group by themselves, and now consolidated into one town.

Zuñi is now reduced to a single village.

The result of the entire difference in the languages of the various groups of Pueblo Indians, and of the facility with which nearly all of them have acquired Spanish, is that if a native of Taos meets one of Santa Clara, or if a party from San Juan visits the great annual festival at Santo Domingo, they have to use the language of Castile for their conversation, instead of the original tongue of any of their people.

After the Spanish occupation the affairs of the Pueblo Indians are naturally included in the general history of the country. Down to the time of the revolution of 1680 it will be found that they were almost always restless and frequently conspiring to drive out the invaders.

But the dozen years of independence, from 1680 to the reconquest by De Vargas, wrought a great change. Under the

Isleta Indian Woman and Boy at Laguna.

Spanish domination they had apparently lost the capacity for self-government. Jealousy and dissension reigned supreme; and when the Spanish expeditions under Cruzate and others penetrated the country, the Pueblos always suffered from divided councils.

After the final re-conquest under De Vargas, we hear no more of Pueblo uprisings or conspiracies. From that time there were almost constant Indian hostilities, but they were with the Apaches, the Comanches, the Utes and the Navajos—the nomadic tribes of the desert and the great plains—and in all of these, the Spaniards and the Pueblo Indians fought side by side against the invaders. Their interests were in common, and they always labored and fought in unison.

So, for the last two hundred years and more they have had no separate history, and whatever affected them will be found in the general consideration of the events of the successive epochs.

CHAPTER IV.

Cabeza De Vaca

The name of Alvar Nuñez Cabeza de Vaca will always be memorable in New Mexican history, as that of the first European who ever set foot upon her soil. He came from the eastward, after a long and tedious journey across a great part of the continent, without any intention to visit the country, either as a conqueror, a missionary, or an explorer, but by a series of accidents which led him through this region while endeavoring, after long years of wanderings and sufferings, to reach some Spanish settlement, where he could again see the faces and hear the language of his countrymen.

The story of his long and perilous journey well illustrates the uncertainties and dangers which characterized the first attempts at exploration.

Cabeza de Vaca had been appointed treasurer of an important expedition undertaken by Panphilo de Narvaez for the conquest and colonization of what was then called Florida, being the whole of the country bordering on the Gulf of Mexico, including all of what now constitutes West Florida, Alabama, Mississippi, Louisiana, Texas, and part of Mexico.

Narvaez obtained from the King of Spain authority to colonize this entire region, of which he was made governor, on condition that he should take no less than two hundred colonists from Spain and found at least two towns, all at his own cost; and he started from San Lucar de Barrameda, in Spain, on the 17th of June, 1527, with five vessels and about 600 men.

From its very commencement ill fortune attended the expedition. At Santo Domingo, no less than 140 men deserted in order to try their fortune on the luxuriant shores of the island. When sailing to Cuba, two of the vessels were destroyed by a tremendous hurricane, the force of the storm being so great that a small boat belonging to one of the ships was found in the branches of a tree a long distance from the coast. Afraid to proceed further, Narvaez wintered on the island, but when he again set sail in the spring continual tempests marked his progress; adverse winds drove his little fleet to the northwest, and on April 12, 1528, they came in sight of land near Tampa Bay in Florida.

Here they landed on the next day, near to an Indian village, but found all of the houses deserted, the inhabitants having fled in the night. On the 14th, the governor raised the Spanish standard and formally took possession of all the surrounding country, in the name of the king, Charles the Fifth.

The Indians whom they met constantly talked of a very rich country to the north, called Apalache, from which they said the pieces of gold which they showed had come. Thither the little army started to march, but met with grave difficulties from the first. The ships, which were ordered to proceed along the coast slowly within easy distance of the land expedition, were soon lost to view, and were never afterwards seen by Narvaez or any of his company. An entire lack of knowledge of the geography of the country caused long delays, and the bays and rivers greatly impeded the journey.

Ten weeks were thus occupied before the welcome sight of Apalache gladdened the eyes of the half-starved and exhausted Spaniards, on June 26th; but instead of a great and rich city they found only a small, poor town without gold or anything of value. Here they remained nearly a month for rest, and then started southward to seek the Gulf at a town called Aute, on Apalachicola Bay. But there an unknown malady attacked them, and many succumbed to its power. As a last resource they determined, if possible, to build rough boats to carry them from the scene of their misfortunes. But no project could seem less possible of execution. They had no tools, no iron, no forge, no rigging; and not a single man who possessed any knowledge of mechanical arts.

Necessity, however, proved, as often before and since, the mother of invention. A bellows was made from a tin pipe and some deer skins; stirrups, spurs, and every article of iron were transformed into nails, axes, and other tools. From the leaves of the palmetto they made a substitute for tow; ropes and rigging were manufacured from the fibre of the same plant and the tails and manes of their horses, while the shirts of the men were given up to be used as sails.

By enormous exertions they succeeded by September 20th in building five boats, and into them the 247 survivors were crowded; the boats being so heavily laden that the men could not move without danger of sinking. What added to the difficulties was that not a single one understood the principles of navigation. Several times, in storms, they were almost overwhelmed, and in passing the mouth of the Mississippi were three days fighting against the mighty current, which threatened to carry them out to sea.

When that was passed, on November third, the vessels were so far separated that none of the others could be seen from that commanded by Cabeza de Vaca, and the whole fleet was never again united. Storm succeeded storm until the provisions were so far reduced that the daily allowance had to be limited to half a handful of raw corn. At length, when all were exhausted, in the darkness of night they were cast ashore on a sandy island on the coast of eastern Texas. Here several were drowned, but the remainder, more dead than alive, were tenderly cared for by the natives, who carried them to their cabins.

Unfortunately, however, their troubles were far from being, even yet, at an end. A severe winter followed, during which sixty-five, of the eighty who had landed, perished. When spring came, twelve of the survivors crossed to the mainland, leaving Cabeza de Vaca and two others who were sick, on the island. In this vicinity, surrounded by Indians, and treated as a slave, the late treasurer remained for six long years, continually looking for means to escape and to travel towards the settlements of his countrymen.

At length, an opportunity offered, and he started inland, and was astonished to hear of three strangers being held by a neighboring tribe, and on meeting them, to find three of his old companions, Alonzo de Castillo, Andres Dorantes, and Estevan, a Barbary negro. These were all held in bondage, to which Vaca was also subjected, and a year and a half elapsed before another opportunity for escape occurred. Then they all proceeded northwesterly far into the interior of Texas, gaining great celebrity among the Indians, as physicians, and being conducted from tribe to tribe with much ceremony, as Superior Beings sent from Heaven for the healing of mankind. Still at times they suffered great privations, traveling entirely naked, and reduced to the verge of starvation. After traversing vast plains, they at length came in sight of mountains, and shortly after reached "a great

Turquoise Mine at Cerrillos, 1880.

river coming from the north;" and then, after crossing rough mountains, devoid of water or food, they were gladdened by the sight of "a very large river, the water of which was breast-high." The first of these streams was undoubtedly the Pecos and the second the Rio Grande.

Soon after, they encountered natives of a very superior character, and for the first time saw "habitations having the appearance and structure of houses." This is the first description that we have of Pueblo Indian towns. Here they found a people entirely different from the nomadic tribes of the Texas plains, wearing garments made of buffalo hide and of cotton, protecting their feet with leather shoes and using the amole or soap weed for cleansing purposes. They had also an abundance of grain, beans, and pumpkins.

Thus westerly the Spaniards traveled, towards the point where they hoped to hear of some of their own conutrymen. They were uniformly well treated among these more civilized Indians, and the people presented them with many fine turquoises, which they said came "from the north" and which were probably the product of the celebrated mine whose vast extent is still a source of wonder, in the Cerrillos district south of Santa Fe.

This mine was worked without any metal tools and is believed to be the largest specimen of aboriginal mining in the United States. The greater part of the summit of the Turquoise Mountain, Mount Chalchuite, has been excavated, by the use of great stone hammers, and tradition says that the rock was also broken by building fires against it and then throwing cold water on the heated surface. In 1879 and 1880 the old workings were reopened and cleaned out by prospectors; and the photograph reproduced in the illustration, was taken at that time.

So Cabeza de Vaca and his companions proceeded through southern New Mexico, northern Chihuahua and Sonora, until they reached a town which they called the Town of Hearts, near which they saw an Indian wearing as ornaments the buckle of a sword belt and the nail of a horseshoe. These things, small in themselves, were to the Spaniards most significant, for they told of the proximity of European settlements; and soon the travelers found themselves in the midst of their countrymen on the shores of the Gulf of California.

This was in the spring of 1536, nearly eight years after their landing in Florida; during fully seven years of this time they had lived altogether among Indians, utterly lost to the civilized world. Years before their unexpected re-appearance they had been mourned as dead.

CHAPTER V

Friar Marcos De Niza

The re-appearance of Cabeza de Vaca, who had long been considered as dead, naturally created great excitement in Mexico. Especially did the descriptions, given with all the exaggeration characteristic of travelers in strange lands, of the great and populous cities, of the civilized country near the Rio Grande, and of the houses four or five stories high, of which they were composed, kindle the adventurous ardor of the Spaniards. They were already greatly interested in that very country, for six years before, in 1530, an Indian, held in slavery by Nuño de Guzman, then governor of New Galicia, brought the first report of the northern region, which he called "The Land of the Seven Cities."

Guzman himself had hoped for an opportunity to proceed to its conquest, but before the time came, he was accused of various political crimes and thrown into prison and, in 1536, Francisco Vasquez Coronado, a man of high position and a chivalric and adventurous spirit, was appointed governor of the province over which he had ruled.

Just then Cabeza de Vaca with his companions arrived in Mexico, with their marvelous stories of the regions to the north. Coronado was charmed and excited by the idea of having such a wonderful field for discovery and conquest on the very border of his province, and determined to lose no time in arranging an expedition which he trusted might be as glorious as those of Cortés and Pizarro. Cabeza de Vaca had already set sail for Spain, but Coronado secured the services of Estevan, the Barbary negro, whose knowledge of the country and of the language of the Indian tribes was considered of great value, and immediately organized an exploring expedition, which he placed in charge of a Franciscan monk, named Marcos de Niza.

His instructions were to proceed immediately and enter the

interior, so as to reach the Land of the Seven Cities, taking Estevan as a guide; to avoid any difficulties with the natives, and to observe and report on all the products of the country, together with the character of the people.

The expedition, which was principally composed of Mexican Indians, started from San Miguel in the Province of Culiacan on the seventh of March, 1539, proceeding northwesterly, parallel to the shore of the Gulf of California, and was everywhere received most hospitably by the natives.

At length they arrived at a desert so extensive that four days were required to cross it, and where so far from ever having seen a white man, the people had not even heard of their existence, and hailed the friar as a celestial visitor, showing him every token of respect and adoration. These people, however, were poor, and the Spaniards eagerly inquired for the large and wealthy cities of which they were in search, and were encouraged by the information that four or five days' journey from the mountains was a great plain where would be found numerous people, living in large towns, who dressed in cotton, and among whom gold abounded. Not only were their household vessels made of this metal, and the walls of their temples plated with it, but the informants particularly mentioned that they "used thin plates of gold to scrape off their sweat," and also that they wore precious green stones suspended from their ears and nostrils.

It being doubtful, however, in which direction it was best to proceed, Friar Marcos concluded to send Estevan in advance with a small party to explore the country, with instructions to send a message whenever he should hear anything of interest. A novel system of communication was agreed on, it being arranged that if the place discovered was not of special importance, the negro should send back a white cross one hand in length; if it were any great matter, one two hands long; and if it were a country greater and better than New Spain, he should send a great cross.

We may imagine, therefore, the excitement occasioned when, only four days after the departure of the advance guard, messengers arrived from Estevan, bringing a great cross as high as a man, and tidings that he had information of a new country which was the greatest in the world.

Accordingly Marcos lost no time in marching on, and soon met numbers of natives who said that they were familiar with the Seven Cities and the Kingdom of Cibola, as they went there to work every summer; and who had much to say of the wealth of the people, of the long cotton garments they wore, and the turquoises almost universally used as ornaments.

Here, also for the first time, the Spaniards heard of the existence of sheep in the country, one of the chiefs informing Marcos, after examining his gray woolen suit, that while at Cibola only cotton cloth was used, at Totonteac were "little animals which furnish the wool from which the same kind of cloth was made."

So he traveled on, crossing deserts and plains, until he arrived at a large town, called Chichilticale, and here the friar was delighted to meet an actual resident of Cibola, whom he describes as far superior to any of the natives whom he had before seen. This man, who was quite aged, described Cibola as a very populous city, with fine streets and market places, with five storied houses built of stone, the gates and pillars being of turquoise, while all the household vessels were of gold.

Marcos was now on the border of a wide desert which was the last to be encountered on the route to Cibola, and a multitude of the people offered to act as an escort to that city.

They started on this expedition on the 9th of May, full of enthusiasm, and thus proceeded for 12 days and nearly to their journey's end, when suddenly they were met by one of the Indians who had accompanied Estevan, nearly exhausted and covered with perspiration.

He told them that on the arrival of the negro at Cibola the inhabitants of the city had taken him and all his company prisoners and put them into a log house just outside the walls. The next morning the narrator, had left the house and gone to a stream near by for water, and while there saw Estevan running away, being pursued by the Cibolans, who were killing his followers as they went. On seeing this, he had hidden himself, and at the first opportunity fled into the desert.

This unexpected news naturally threw the followers of Marcos into consternation, but they journeyed on until within a single day's march of Cibola, when they met two more of the Indians who had accompanied Estevan, wounded and bleeding. These told the same story of the capture and attempted escape of the negro and his party. They had been pursued by the Cibolans, who killed many and wounded all, so that they believed they were the only survivors of the entire expedition. This news, which concerned the sons and brothers of those who formed the escort of Marcos, roused them to frenzy, not only against the men of Cibola but against the friar who had brought this great calamity upon them.

All his persuasion could not induce them to go a foot nearer the city where such destruction had taken place; and Marcos had to content himself with taking observations of it from a distance. For that purpose he went to an adjacent elevation from which he could look into it, and in his report says that "it maketh show to be a fair city and better seated than any I have seen in these parts. The houses are builded in order, all made of stone, with divers stories and flat roofs. The people are somewhat white, they wear apparel and lie in beds; their weapons are bows; they have emeralds and other jewels, although they esteem none so much as turquoise, wherewith they adorn the walls and the porches of their houses and their apparel and dresses, and they use them instead of money. They use vessels of gold and silver, whereof there is greater use and of more abundance than in Peru."

Having thus viewed from afar the Promised Land into which he could not enter, Friar Marcos set up a slender cross and formally proclaimed that he took possession of the province in the name of the viceroy and of the king of Spain; and then hastened to overtake his escort, which was returning with a rapidity inspired by fear; but found so much feeling aroused against him among the natives that he was glad to escape from them by swift traveling. In due time he reached the Mexican towns and made a report which by its extraordinary exaggerations of the wealth and importance of the Land of the Seven Cities created a great excitement and swiftly led to the celebrated expedition of Coronado.

CHAPTER VI

Coronado

The reports brought back by Friar Marcos to Mexico were so much beyond what had been hoped, that both the viceroy and Governor Coronado were eager for the conquest of the new El Dorado beyond the desert.

It was immediately determined to organize an expedition, of which Coronado was very properly named as commander. The most chivalrous and enterprising cavaliers of New Spain flocked to his standard, so that the troop of Spaniards which finally started on the great march was the most brilliant that had ever been gathered in the New World.

In order that the commander might not gain ill will in the selection of officers, the viceroy performed this duty himself, knowing that all would willingly submit tö his decision. He chose for standard-bearer Pedro de Tobar, a young cavalier, and appointed as Maestro de Campo, Lope de Samaniego, a chevalier well worthy of this position. The captains were Tristan de Arellano, Pedro de Guevara, Garcia Lopez de Cardenas, Rodrigo Maldonado, Diego Lopez, and Diego Gutierrez, captain of cavalry. The commander of the infantry was Pablo de Melgosa, and the chief of artillery Hernando de Alvarado.

All told, the army consisted of 400 Spaniards and 800 Indian soldiers, and it was fully organized at Compostela, the capital of New Galicia, in the spring of 1540. To show his great interest, the viceroy himself came to the city and held a grand review of the troops, and accompanied the expedition for two days in order to encourage it to the fullest extent. As soon as he departed, the holiday aspect disappeared and the real work of the march began. Many soon found that they had brought far too much baggage and were glad to give away superfluous articles; others, who had been brought up to lives of luxury, found themselves compelled to perform work to which they were far from accustomed. Still, all pressed forward eagerly towards the wonderful "Land of the Seven Cities," which was to bring to each one wealth and honor.

At Culiacan, Coronado's impatience to reach the field of conquest became so great that he decided to press on in advance of the main body of the army; and so, taking Friar Marcos as guide, with fifty horsemen and a few soldiers on foot, he started on, leaving the remainder under the command of Don Tristan de Arellano. The governor proceeded rapidly over the road traveled by Marcos two years before, and the troops were full of enthusiasm until they reached the town on the edge of the desert of which the friar had given such a glowing account, and which was called Chichilticale. But here came a great disappointment; for instead of the flourishing city they had been led to expect, they found but one single dwelling and that in a ruinous condition. This building is readily identified, being that now known as the Casa Grande of Arizona.

Although somewhat depressed, Coronado determined still to press on, and so marched into the great desert which he was 15 days in crossing. At the end of that time, he was gladdened by the sight of a stream of water, which from its reddish color the Spaniards called Vermejo, and which is now named Colorado Chiquito (Little Red).

Two days after, Coronado and his little army arrived in sight of the famous city of which they had heard so much; but what was their astonishment to find that instead of a great capital, it was but a small town containing not over two hundred warriors, situated on a great rock, and difficult of approach. It was true that the houses were three or four stories high, but they were small and badly arranged.

Coronado by signs made overtures of friendship, but the Cibolans prepared to resist an attack. An assault soon followed, the Spaniards charging with loud cries of "Santiago," and forced the Indians to fly to the shelter of the town. The Spaniards followed, but as the only place of ascent was steep and dangerous, they met with considerable loss. Showers of stones were hailed upon them, and Coronado himself was struck to the ground and narrowly escaped death. Still they pressed on, and finally the discipline of trained warriors, together with the advantage of fire arms, prevailed; and the Christians marched in triumph through the streets. This town is now called by the Indians "Hawaikuh."

Here Coronado remained for a considerable time, waiting for the arrival of his main army. The Province of Cibola—which is the modern Zuñi—contained seven towns in all, all well governed by the older men. The people were orderly and industrious and exemplary in their habits. They treated the Spaniards with hospitality and in return Coronado prevented any outrages being committed by his soldiers. At length the main army arrived, fatigued from their march, and the southern Indians suffering from the cold and snow to which they were not accustomed; but otherwise they were in good condition.

While they were resting, Coronado sent a small detachment under Don Pedro de Tobar to visit the province called Tusayan, about twenty-five leagues to the northwest, in which he was told there were seven cities similar to those of Cibola. So swiftly did this expedition march that it arrived in the night under the very walls of the nearest of these cities, and the first notice that the inhabitants had of danger was the sight of the Spaniards in their midst at early dawn. Some parleying ensued, followed by an attack by the Spaniards on the natives and terminating as usual in the submission of the latter; and within a short time all of the towns acknowledged the authority of the strangers.

This province, which is the modern Moqui or Hopi, was undoubtedly the Totonteac of which Marcos gave such glowing accounts. It consisted of seven villages, governed, as were those of Cibola, by councils of aged men. The people were industrious, raising large quantities of corn, and making well tanned leather.

Here Don Pedro was told of a great river to the westward, on which a race of giants dwelt, and was so much impressed with the description of its size and depth, that Coronado sent another expedition, consisting of twelve horsemen under Don Garcia Lopez de Cardenas, to search for it. This party marched westerly for twenty days through an uninhabited country, until at length they beheld—first of all Europeans—what we now know as the Grand Cañon of the Colorado. For three days they traveled along its side, seeking for a place to descend into the cañon, but were forced to return without accomplishing that feat.

While this expedition was absent, there came to visit Coronado a deputation from a province far to the eastward, called Cicuic, headed by their young chief, who on account of his long mustaches was called by the Spaniards "Bigotes." He said that the news of the arrival of the white men had reached his country, two hundred miles away, and they had come to offer their friendship and services. As this afforded a good opportunity for exploration, Coronado directed Alvarado with twenty men to accompany Bigotes on his return and to gain all the knowledge possible of the country. Accordingly, they set out with the deputation from Cicuic, and at the end of five days came to the pueblo of Acoma—a town situated on the summit of a great rock, whose sides are so perpendicular that ascent is impossible except in one place, where artificial steps have been made. Here the people were found to have great quantities of pottery, bread, corn, piñons, etc., of all of which they generously presented supplies to the Spaniards.

Without delay, however, Alvarado continued on with Bigotes, and in three days came to the province of Tihuex (pronounced Tee-wesh), containing twelve villages in all. This province stretched along the Rio Grande for thirty or forty miles, from the vicinity of the present Albuquerque to that of San Felipe; the town of Tihuex itself being near Bernalillo, and very possibly identical with the Puará of later narratives.

Five days more brought the little expedition, with Bigotes, to the home of the latter at Cicuic, a large and handsome town, built in terrace form around a square, with houses four stories in height, and strongly fortified. Here the Spaniards were received with special hospitality, as the guests of the chief; and remained for some time, until the main army had arrived at Tihuex.

This town of Cicuic (pronounced See-coo-eek), which was the largest in New Mexico, and at that time, in the whole of the present United States, is easily identified as the more modern Pecos. The word is variously spelled Cicuic, Cicuyc, Cicuique, Acuique, etc., and by mistaking the final "c" for an "e," appeared in a French translation as Cicuye, and has been copied in that erroneous form by many recent writers.

While here, Alvarado met a man whose statements had much

to do with the future of the expedition. This was a native of the far east, who was held as a servant at Cicuic, and who from his oriental appearance was always called by the Spaniards, "The Turk," to the exclusion of any other name. As soon as he met Alvarado, he began to urge him to march over the plains to a wonderful country, which he described as abounding in gold and silver; and whose chief city was called Quivira. So glowing were his accounts, that the Spanish captain felt that it was a waste of time to explore a country whose only wealth was in buffaloes; and so, without going further, he hastened back to Coronado, to tell of the great news he had received, taking "The Turk" with him.

In the meantime, the Spanish army, in accordance with the suggestion of Alvarado, had made Tihuex its winter quarters, taking possession of the houses and treating the inhabitants with much harshness; a poor return for their recent hospitality. Coronado himself waited at Cibola for re-enforcements under Tristan de Arellano, and then marched on to Tihuex, taking a route through a province of eight villages, called Tutahaco.

When he arrived in Tihuex Alvarado lost no time in bringing "The Turk" before him, and the latter was now even more extravagant than before in his descriptions of the east. He said that in that country was a river two leagues in width, containing fish the size of a horse, and navigated by great vessels, in the stern of which the nobles sat under canopies surrounded by every luxury. All his descriptions ended with the statement that the commonest vessels in this far-off land were of silver, and all the table utensils of gold.

Strange to say, these stories were believed, without a doubt; and such confidence was placed in the Turk that those opposing him were distrusted. Even Bigotes and the cacique of Cicuic were seized and imprisoned, on a false statement of this imposter.

This naturally caused great indignation among the natives, which was enhanced by the harshness of Spanish officers in collecting cotton goods for clothing for their troops, and by other outrages. The result was a general uprising, in which the Indians wisely maintained a defensive attitude within their almost impregnable houses. The Spanish attacks resulted only in loss, until some Indian allies dug underground passages to some of the houses, and by kindling fires, so filled them with smoke, that the inmates were compelled to come out.

All through the winter, hostilities continued, culminating in the siege of Tihuex, which lasted no less than fifty days, with considerable loss on both sides, until the inhabitants were compelled to abandon the town for want of water, and most of them perished in the river or by the hands of the Spaniards. While this siege was in progress, Coronado visited Cicuic in order to regain the friendship of the people, and by restoring their cacique to liberty and promising soon to liberate Bigotes, succeeded in that design.

The whole army was impatient to start on its march to the far east, of which "The Turk" had given such vivid descriptions, and especially to the rich city of Quivira, which was the special object of their ambition. The winter, however, was an unusually long and severe one, so that it was not until May 5, 1541, that the march from Tihuex actually commenced. At Cicuic, Bigotes was returned to his people, and presented to Coronado a young Indian named Xabe, who was a native of Quivira itself, to assist as guide on the expedition.

After crossing some mountains, they came to a large river too deep to ford, and where consequently they were detained four days in constructing a bridge; after which they marched for ten days more over a rough and hilly country, when they arrived at the border of the plains and soon saw the camp of a nomadic tribe called "Querechos," who lived in tents of buffalo skins. The country now traversed was the great plain east of the mountains in New Mexico, which they found covered with enormous droves of buffaloes. Occasionally they came to great ravines in one of which they found an encampment of Indians, who reported that they had met Cabeza de Vaca seventeen years before.

Thus the army traveled in a general northeasterly direction, through a level country, well supplied with fruit, daily losing faith in the glowing stories of the Turk as they heard the plain statements of Indians, whom he had no opportunity to consult in advance, until they had been thirty-seven days on the route. Provisions were now running low, and altogether the situation was so serious that it was finally determined that the general with thirty horsemen and six foot soldiers should proceed in search of Quivira; while the main body of the army, after waiting a reasonable time for advices, should return to Tihuex under Tristan de Arellano. The soldiers, who idolized Coronado, objected strenuously to this programme, but it was nevertheless carried out; the Turk being taken with the exploring party, in chains, as punishment for what were now recognized as his false statements.

The little party traveled rapidly, but still it required forty-eight days to make the journey across the plains to Quivira. This celebrated city was found just to the east of a great river and appears to have consisted of a succession of villages situated on small streams which flowed into that river from the east. It was certainly great in extent, but as far as wealth was concerned, it was an entire disappointment. So far from possessing great quantities of the precious metals, the people appeared to have no knowledge, whatever, of either gold or silver; indeed no metals were seen at all, except a plate of copper which the ruler wore upon his breast, and which was very highly esteemed by all the people.

Nothing could exceed the indignation of the Spaniards at the Turk when these facts became known; and he, seeing that nothing was to be accomplished by further deception, acknowledged that he had given them false information at the request of the people of Cicuic, who wished the Spaniards to be led astray on the plain, so that they would perish there. It is not strange, under the circumstances, that Coronado's officers promptly strangled the imposter, nor need we be surprised that the general quickly turned back from this city, which failed to meet the demand for gold which actuated most of the adventurous explorers of those days.

At the farthest point that he reached in exploring the city, he erected a great cross with this inscription, "Francisco Vasquez de Coronado, Commander of an expedition, arrived at this place." The houses were generally circular, with roofs of straw, so arranged as to be water-tight; and outside, on top, many of them had a kind of cupola.

The exact situation of Quivira has been the subject of much controversy. The weight of opinion seems to be that it was somewhere in northeastern Kansas, on the banks of a considerable river, but whether as far east as the Missouri or on a smaller stream is uncertain. The description given shows it to have been not unlike other settlements of Indians in that section of the country, none of which were very permanent in character.

While Coronado and his little company had been making their long journey across the plains, the main army under Arellano had returned to Tihuex. From there several expeditions were sent out; one up the Jemez river as far as Jemez, and still further north to the large pueblo of Braba, easily recognizable as the present pueblo of Taos; and another exploring the country along the Rio Grande, to the south, a distance of 80 leagues, and discovering four towns not before visited, probably including the present Socorro and San Antonio.

In August, Coronado and his little party returned to Cicuic, having traveled from Quivira by a better route in but forty days; and continued to Tihuex to prepare for a grand expedition to be undertaken in the coming spring, not only to the land of Quivira, but to regions far beyond.

But an accident changed the whole course of procedure. While Coronado was engaged at his favorite game of running at a ring, in company with Don Rodrigo Maldonado, the saddle girth broke and he was thrown to the ground immediately in front of the horse of the latter and received a kick in the head which well-night proved fatal. He was confined to his bed for a considerable time, a feeling of despondency spread throughout the army, and a petition was handed to the general, asking an abandonment of the expedition. Coronado, himself, wearied with sickness, promptly acceded to the request.

Early in April, 1542, the army set out on its homeward march. Two missionaries, Juan de Padilla and Luis de Escalona, especially desired to remain and labor among the natives; and consequently were left. The former, it is said, was martyred close to Quivira; and the other doubtless shared his fate. At Cibola, a number of the Mexican Indians, pleased with the country, concluded to remain; and here several of them were met forty years afterwards by Espejo.

As soon as the Mexican settlements were reached, the forces began to melt away, the men returning to their homes by the shortest routes, so that when Coronado arrived at the city of Mexico he could barely muster a hundred men. His lack of success caused him to be coldly received by the viceroy, and soon after he was deprived of his governorship, and never again takes a prominent place in history.

CHAPTER VII

Friar Ruiz and Espejo

Almost forty years passed after the expedition of Coronado, before any further attempts were made to penetrate into New Mexico.

The next expedition was not military in its character, nor did it have the gratification of ambition or cupidity for its object; but it was undertaken by missionaries, whose sole object was the spread of the Gospel.

Agustin Ruiz or Rodriguez, a Franciscan friar, laboring at San Bartolomé, in northeastern Mexico, heard, in the year 1581, of great provinces along the Rio Grande to the north, which the Spaniards had never visited, and he determined at all hazards to penetrate their country and carry to them a knowledge of christianity. Two of his brothers in the order of St. Francis, Francisco Lopez and Juan de Santa Maria, resolved to accompany him; and they were provided with an escort of nine soldiers under a captain named Chamuscado. Eight Indians and one half-breed accompanied the missionaries as servants; and the expedition left San Bartolomé, June 6, 1581.

After a long northerly march of about five hundred miles they at length arrived among the Pueblo Indians of the Rio Grande Valley, and reached a town called Puará, or Puaray, which was situated about eight miles north of the present site of Albuquerque. At this point the soldiers absolutely refused to go further, on account of the danger. The friars endeavored to persuade them to continue the journey; and the soldiers in turn tried to persuade the friars to retrace their steps to Mexico. Neither would yield, and so they separated: the soldiers of the crown returned to the ease and security of their garrison life, and the Soldiers of the Cross went forward, braving danger and death, to carry the words of salvation to the heathen regions beyond.

The friars continued as far north as Galisteo, and then concluded to send one of their number back to Mexico in order to bring more brethren into the field. Brother Juan de Santa Maria was selected for the journey. He proceeded directly south toward El Paso, but on his way, when near the pueblo of San Pablo, he was killed by the Indians, while quietly resting under a tree. The other two settled in Puará in order to learn the Indian language together, but were soon separated by the murder of Brother Lopez who was violently struck on the head, while engaged in prayer.

Friar Ruiz was now alone, and while he keenly felt his isolation and realized his danger, he resolutely determined to remain at his post. But his death was certain, for the destruction of all the missionaries had been decreed by the Pueblo authorities, and but a few days elapsed before he likewise received a martyr's crown.

Thus ended this peaceful expedition into New Mexico by the death of the three devoted men who undertook the work. But their labors were not in vain, for the proverb that "the blood of the martyrs is the seed of the Church" was illustrated by the baptism within fifty years of over 34,000 Indians, and the erection of over forty churches.

Espejo's Expedition.

No sooner had the Franciscans in Mexico heard from the returning soldiers of the peril in which the three missionaries were left, than they made an urgent appeal that relief might be sent. This touched the heart of Don Antonio de Espejo, a wealthy Spaniard engaged in mining at Santa Barbara, who generously offered himself and his fortune to the work.

Don Antonio was a man of great energy of character, and in a short time all was in readiness. On the tenth day of November, 1582, the expedition commenced its march from San Bartolomé, and moved directly north, through the present state of Chihuahua, toward New Mexico. Here the first province entered was called Humanos, and it appeared to have been visited by Cabeza de Vaca in his journey across the continent, as the people mentioned having been taught certain things by three white men and a negro,

Two other provinces were successively passed through, in both of which the people were well-dressed in chamois skins and cotton clothes; and then the army had to traverse a long stretch of uninhabited country, and afterwards found themselves in beautiful groves of cottonwoods, and entered an important province situated in the vicinity of the present pueblo of Isleta. The houses here were four stories high and well-constructed, and the people were very industrious, raising large quantities of cotton in addition to the ordinary cereals. This province contained ten towns.

Proceeding up the valley, the Spaniards soon came near to Puará and then for the first time heard of the death of the three friars. They were naturally much grieved to find that so far as saving their lives was concerned, the expedition was in vain. As much was heard, however, of the richness of the surrounding country, it was determined to make brief explorations in various directions before returning to Mexico. The first of these was made by Espejo himself with only two men, who traveled easterly for two days and found a province on the border of the great buffalo plains, containing eleven towns and forty thousand inhabitants, where the people had great herds of cattle, and the wealthier classes had considerable gold and silver in their houses.

This encouraged him to undertake a more important expedition. He proceeded northerly up the Rio Grande to the province of the Queres Indians, where he found five villages, the population of which he estimated at 14,000. He then traveled westerly to a province called Cunames and which also contained five towns, of which the pueblo of Zia was the most important. This town was at that time much larger than at present, and was built around eight plazas, the houses being the best that the Spaniards had seen during their expedition, stuccoed and painted with many colors. The people were well advanced in civilization and among other articles showed curious and beautiful mantles, which attracted much attention from their visitors. Continuing westerly, Espejo next found a people whom he calls Amies and who are easily recognizable as being the Jemez Indians. They lived in seven towns, and their number was computed to be thirty thousand.

Fifteen leagues farther on the little expedition arrived at the pueblo of Acoma; and its commanding position particularly impressed the Spaniards. ' Throughout the whole of this trip Espejo was received with great hospitality, but in this respect the people of Acoma exceeded their neighbors, entertaining the Spaniards with their national games and dances and bringing presents of every kind.

After remaining three days at Acoma, Espejo proceeded directly to Zuñi, which he distinctly identifies as the place called Cibola by the preceding Spanish writers, and, on arriving at that important pueblo, was surprised to find three of the Mexican Indians who had remained there for the forty years since they were left by Coronado. These men, whose names were Andres, Gaspar and Antonio, had almost entirely forgotten their native language during their long sojourn at Cibola, but their delight on seeing the Spaniards can be imagined. They were anxious to be of any service possible, and so informed Espejo of a rich country in which the precious metals abounded and which was situated far to the westward on a great lake.

This story was sufficiently alluring to induce Espejo to visit it, which he did with nine soldiers, leaving the remainder of his little company at Zuñi. After traveling twenty-eight leagues he came to the modern Moqui, whose population, with his usual over-estimate, he placed at 50,000. He spent some days here, and then he proceeded on the quest for the land of gold and silver. In this he was not without success, as he gives an enthusiastic description of a mine containing a vein of silver of remarkable width from which he took rich specimens with his own hands. This was in a mountainous region, a little north of the modern Prescott, as his journey did not extend as far as the Colorado river, although he heard much of it from the Indian guides who endeavored to excite his interest by telling him that it was eight leagues in width!

But Espejo was now anxious to return, and so journeyed back to Zuñi where he found Father Beltran and the soldiers left with him, in good health, but impatient to see Mexico again, and so he allowed them to return to their homes, leaving him with but eight companions in his further explorations.

He now turned northward and followed the banks of the Rio Grande until he found a province on the east of the river containing about 25,000 people, well-dressed and living in houses many stories in height. This was in a mountainous country, which he called Hubates, where there were many evergreens, and probably included that part of New Mexico extending from Tesuque and Nambé to Santa Clara and San Juan. While here he heard of the towns of the Tanos, which he says were only one day's travel distant, and he proceeded to visit them, going as far as the pueblo of Pecos. The population of the Tanos province he places, from information received, at 40,000, although he did not visit all of the towns. Contrary to his usual experience, he was not received with cordiality by these people, who refused to allow him to enter their towns; and this seems to have led to a feeling of fear of what might occur if the Indians became really hostile.

From his extended explorations Espejo was well satisfied of the wealth of the country, but he concluded that a much larger expedition was necessary to insure success in colonization or in conquest. So he decided to return to Mexico and look to the future for an opportunity of utilizing the store of information as to this new country, which he called New Mexico.

Instead of retracing his route in the Rio Grande Valley, he was induced by the advice of guides to follow the untried path down the Pecos river, and thus was the first European to explore the course of that stream. He calls it the "River of Cows," because the buffaloes were so numerous everywhere. Starting in the beginning of July he followed it to the point where it enters the Rio Grande, and then, crossing the latter, proceeded by way of the Conchos to his home in New Biscay, where he arrived on September 20, 1583; and wrote an interesting "relacion" of his journey to the viceroy of New Spain, who transmitted it to the king.

CHAPTER VIII

Attempts at Colonization, 1585-1598

The discoveries of Espejo attracted universal interest, and his narration was immediately published in Spain and Rome, and soon appeared in many languages and editions. The immediate result of the news of these discoveries was to arouse in several ambitious breasts a desire to conquer and colonize the regions thus made known. To do this legally required an authorization either from the king or from the viceroy of New Spain, and applicants in considerable numbers soon addressed themselves to those high dignitaries.

The most natural applicant for this opportunity for fame and conquest was Espejo himself, and he made his appeal directly to the king, forwarding a full account of the success which had attended his previous efforts with a proposed plan of operations for a new expedition. For reasons which we cannot now understand, but which had their origin probably in the unfriendliness of the viceroy, this proposition was not accepted.

About the same time, Don Francisco Diaz de Vargas, alguazil mayor of the city of Puebla de los Angeles, made a similar application. Other aspirants for the honors of leadership were Don Cristobal Martin of the city of Mexico, and Juan Bautista de Lomas, who had been very successful in mining adventures in New Galicia, but again a refusal was the answer which came from Spain.

CASTANO DE SOSA

At length in the year 1590 Don Gaspar Castaño de Sosa, who was lieutenant-governor of the province of Nueva Leon, concluded to act on the authority he already possessed, of colonizing the vicinity of the province in which he was holding office without further formality.

He started from the town of Almaden on July 27, 1590, with a party of 170 persons, including some women and children, and an ample supply of provisions. He crossed the Rio Grande to the Pecos and then proceeded up the valley of the latter until the advance guard of his expedition arrived at the pueblo of Pecos itself a few days before Christmas. This party was kindly received in the first place, but, after passing the night in the pueblo, they were suddenly attacked and driven out of town. Immediate information of this event was sent to Castaño, who was encamped with the larger portion of his expedition at a point lower down on the Pecos, called Urraca. Without delay he marched against the town and made an attack on New Year's Day, which resulted in the capture of the place; but the Indians, as had been their custom ever since their earliest conflicts with the Spaniards, entirely deserted the town on the second night and retired to the mountains. Castaño found an immense accumulation of corn, stored away according to the Pueblo custom, for any emergency that might occur, and which the Spaniards estimated to amount to 30,000 fanegas. A portion of this was sent to Urraca, and Castaño then started to explore the remainder of the country.

He first marched northwesterly as far as the present pueblo of Taos and returned down the valley of the Rio Grande, crossing to two pueblos situated on the west side of the river, and afterwards re-crossing to another on the east, which may have been San Ildefonso. Continuing down the valley, they found four towns very near together, three of which were probably Cochití, Santo Domingo, and San Felipe.

Having visited twenty of the Indian villages and explored the greater part of the Upper Rio Grande Valley, Castaño concluded to establish a permanent colony to which all of his party should be brought. This he established at San Marcos and on the eighteenth of February, 1591, all of the outlying parties had arrived and arrangements were made for the erection of permanent buildings. Attention was then given to the mineral riches of the country, and exploring parties were sent out in various directions, which included the modern mining districts of the Cerrillos, the Ortiz, and the Tuerto Mountains.

As the country to the south had not yet been explored, another

ATTEMPTS AT COLONIZATION. 57

expedition was now sent down the river to the province of the Tihuas, and here they visited no less than nine Indian towns, besides seeing five others, part on the east and part on the west side of the river.

Thus within less than a year Castaño had visited nearly all of the inhabited portion of New Mexico, and, without the loss of a single man, had obtained the control of no less than thirty-three pueblos; and we might well have dated the permanent colonization of New Mexico from this time and have hailed Castaño as being the leader in its occupation, had not the jealousy of the authorities of Spain and Mexico brought this expedition to an untimely end. For at this point Castaño received news that there was another party of Spaniards which was not far distant. He hailed this information with joy as he supposed that they were re-enforcements, but was surprised to find that they consisted of fifty soldiers under Captain Juan Morlete who had been sent with orders to arrest him for having undertaken his expedition without proper authority. He made no resistance but allowed himself to be placed in irons and re-conducted with his whole party to Mexico, thus abandoning the labors which had so nearly resulted in complete success.

BONILLA AND HUMANA

One other attempt at exploration deserves attention before we come to the actual colonization of the country. About 1595, a party was sent out by the governor of New Biscay to punish certain Indians who had been committing depredations, the expedition being commanded by a Portuguese named Francisco Leiva Bonilla. After he had accomplished his mission, the ambitious Bonilla concluded, if possible, to reach the ever-alluring Quivira. He marched easterly across the buffalo plains toward the object of his aspirations; but a quarrel arose between himself and one of his lieutenants named Juan de Humaña, which resulted in the death of the captain and in the assumption of the command by Humaña. This man, whose ambition equaled that of his late commander, succeeded in reaching a point on the great grassy prairie of Southern Kansas or Northern Oklahoma, which was ever after referred to as the "Matanza." The Indians of that region set fire to the grass which surrounded his camp, and then, just before daylight, rushed upon the half-awakened Spaniards and destroyed the entire party with the exception of one mulatto girl and a man named Alonzo Sanchez. A Mexican Indian, named Jusepe, deserted the party before the catastrophe and went to New Mexico, where he was seen years afterwards by Oñate and became of service as an interpreter.

CHAPTER IX

The Conquest by Oñate

After all these fruitless efforts, success was at last attained under the leadership of Don Juan de Oñate. This cavalier, who was a wealthy citizen of Zacatecas, was so strongly excited by the reports from the new El Dorado that he made application in 1595 to Viceroy Velasco for authorization to colonize the country, offering to take with him at least 200 soldiers at his own expense. The permission was given in due time, on condition that the colonization should be completed within five years.

Oñate lost no time in organizing his expedition, and everything promised successful results, until the arrival of a new viceroy in the place of Velasco changed the aspect of affairs, and every obstacle possible was placed in the way of the expedition.

The final authorization from the king was not received till late in 1597, and meanwhile the little army had become so reduced that barely 130 could be mustered for final inspection. To meet the requirements of his contract Oñate arranged that eighty additional troops should follow as soon as possible, and started on his march from San Bartolomé on January 20, 1598.

The little army was accompanied by a large number of families for colonization, and included ten Franciscan friars. Among the officers were a number of high distinction, including the two nephews of Oñate, Juan and Vicente de Saldivar, and Captain Gaspar Villagrá, a gallant soldier and the poet-historian of the expedition, to whom posterity is indebted for the most extensive epic ever written on early American history. This poem, entitled *Historia de la Nueva Mexico*, contains 33 cantos, and gives a graphic narrative of all the events of the colonization from first to last.

Proceeding slowly, on account of the heavy wagons, the column crossed the Conchos, and marched through Chihuahua until, on

April 20, it reached the Rio Grande about twenty-five miles below El Paso. On the 30th a halt was made in a beautiful grove on the west bank; and here, Oñate raised the royal standard of Spain, and formally took possession of New Mexico and all the adjoining provinces, for God and the king, and for himself as governor. The festivities ended at night with the performance of a comedy written for the occasion by Captain Farfan, which may be considered the introduction of the drama into the southwest.

Four days later, on May 4, 1598, the expedition crossed the Rio Grande at El Paso del Norte, and proceeded up the east side of the river. On the 25th, they were near Mesilla, and there Oñate selected 50 or 60 of the best mounted men, and with them pressed forward in advance of the main body of the colonists in search of food, which was becoming scarce. Three days later he arrived at the first of the Pueblo Indian towns, which were three in number. The first was near the present San Marcial; the second was called Qualicu or Senecu, and is the San Antonio of to-day; and the third was called Teipana. In all of them they were hospitably received by the natives, and at Teipana they obtained such an amount of corn that on account of this timely succor the town was named Socorro.

Resuming the march, the governor and his party reached Puará, on June 28, and on July 11 came to the beautiful valley at the junction of the Chama with the Rio Grande, where he found the pueblo of Caypa on the eastern bank of the river. The inhabitants of this place showed so much kindness that the Spaniards added to the new name of San Juan the words "de los Caballeros" (of the gentlemen), and the title San Juan de los Caballeros has continued to this day.

The beauty and fertility of the valley, in addition to this warm reception, struck the attention of the Spaniards, and they determined to make this the official center of the new kingdom. The very next day, July 12, 1598, they commenced the building of the new capital on the west side of the Rio Grande between that river and the Chama, in a place called Yunque, and named the infant city San Gabriel; and its ruins may still be seen from the windows of the passing train, at the modern station of Chamita. This date, July 12, 1598, may be considered as the birthday of European settlement in New Mexico; and its anniversary should be celebrated in the southwest, just as the date of the landing of the Pilgrim Fathers on Plymouth Rock, on December 21, 1620, is annually observed wherever the memory of the founders of New England is venerated. In 1898, the three hundredth anniversary was fittingly celebrated, on the ground, by the New Mexico Historical Society.

While awaiting the arrival of the slow caravan of his colonists at San Gabriel, Oñate visited Picuris and Taos; and then, turning southward, rode to San Ildefonso, and thence to Pecos, where he arrived on the 25th of July. Returning by the way of Santo Domingo, he traveled through Zia and Jemez, visiting some hot sulphur springs on the route; and again found himself at San Gabriel August 10th.

The long line of colonists was now arriving, and the last were in the new city by the 18th; and then all hands were called on to aid in the building of the church—the first Christian temple in New Mexico. It did not need to be very large to meet present requirements; but, if its size were small, the ceremonies of its dedication were made as elaborate as possible in order to impress the minds of the natives. These ceremonies took place on September 8th, and at their conclusion there was a dramatic representation of a conflict between the Christians and the Moors, in which the former by the timely aid of St. James were gloriously victorious, to the great satisfaction of all the audience, both white and red.

Advantage was taken of the presence of large numbers of Indians to hold a great meeting of the Spanish officials and ecclesiastics and the representatives of the pueblos, under the grandiloquent title of "Universal Meeting of all the Earth." On this occasion their obligations both to Cross and Crown were elaborately explained to the Indians, and they acknowledged the sovereignty of the Spanish king, and agreed to receive the Franciscans as their religious guides; though at the same time they suggested that the Spaniards certainly would not wish them to profess a belief which they did not yet comprehend.

Having attended to all these ceremonials, Oñate resumed his series of rapid journeys, by which he was determined to visit every portion of the new kingdom with the least possible delay.

While Vicente de Saldivar was sent with a party of fifty men to explore the great buffalo plains to the east, Oñate himself started south to make a personal visit to the pueblos east of the Rio Grande in the Salinas country, at Abó, Tabira, etc., and into the land of the Jumanos; and then started on the longest of his expeditions, extending not only to Acoma and Zuñi, but also far into Arizona to the land of the Moquis.

He was received everywhere with apparent cordiality, all of the pueblos accepting the Spanish sovereignty without objection; although it afterwards appeared that at Acoma a number of leaders had formed a conspiracy to kill the governor by luring him into an estufa. The leader of this party was Zutucapan, an eloquent chieftain, who was determined to destroy the invaders, and who soon inflamed the minds of the people and controlled their actions.

The wished-for opportunity soon arrived. Oñate had left orders at San Gabriel, that as soon as Vicente Saldivar returned from his exploration, his brother Juan should march with such soldiers as could be spared, to reinforce the governor on his western tour. He accordingly started on November 18th, following the route taken by Oñate by the way of Acoma. Here the Indians received him cordially and invited his little troup to the summit of their high mesa; but no sooner were they scattered in various houses than a sudden attack was made. The Spaniards fought with desperation for fully three hours, but were greatly over-matched by numbers; finally Zutucapan succeeded in killing Captain Saldivar himself with a terrific blow of his macana, and the five surviving Spaniards threw themselves down from the cliff as the only chance of escape. By what seemed a miracle, four survived the tremendous fall. They sent a swift messenger to inform Oñate of the catastrophe, and he speedily returned to San Gabriel to take measures to punish the rebellious pueblos.

It was plain that this had to be done without delay, no matter at what sacrifice, or the whole country would rise against them. Yet the enterprise was a most dangerous and difficult one, on account of the almost impregnable character of the mesa of Acoma, which is composed of two perpendicular cliffs, connected by a narrow ridge, and to each cliff there is but one

THE CONQUEST BY ONATE. 63

steep, almost inaccessible entrance. A dozen resolute men, even if armed only with stones, could hold the main approach against the world in the days before artillery changed the whole science of warfare.

The enterprise was entrusted to Vicente de Saldivar, brother of the captain who had fallen, and he was given command of a little army of only seventy men, but each one selected for his bravery and prowess.

On the 21st of January, 1599, they came in sight of the great cliff, and could see the crowd of warriors upon the summit. Its perpendicular walls seemed an insurmountable barrier that made capture impossible. But what might not succumb to force might be gained by cunning, and Don Vicente laid his plans accordingly.

In the darkness of the night, with a dozen chosen comrades, he concealed himself in the clefts of the smaller cliff. Then at break of day all the remainder of the little army made a fierce attack on the main entrance to the larger mesa. There the Indians were prepared and soon hurled back the advance of the Spaniards.

But meanwhile, all unseen, Saldivar's little band had gained the top of the other cliff and stood upon a level with their foes. Then came a fierce struggle at the narrow pass. Everywhere it was a hand-to-hand struggle; and to fall on either cliff or on the narrow ridge between, meant swift destruction on the jagged sides of the rocky mesas or in the abyss below. Night came but brought no rest; and with the dawn of another day, came only a renewal of the conflict.

The Indians outnumbered the Spaniards more than ten to one, but the latter were clad in mail and carried the deadly firearms which could deal death beyond the reach of the macana. It was a battle full of deeds of valor and of daring. All that day the fight went on—and still the struggle was not decided.

The third day came, and the Spaniards pressed the Indians back into their long line of terraced houses, and then these became a mass of flame, and the inmates had to choose between two frightful kinds of death. In desperation they killed themselves or rushed out and threw themselves down the cliffs to sure destruction. In all history there is no more desperate battle, nor ever one on such a dizzy height. Of over 3,000 Indians only six hundred survived, and they were compelled to leave their home on the great rock and settle on the plain.

The moral effect of this great victory was immense. There was no longer any danger of opposition. Every pueblo acknowledged the Spanish authority. The conquest of New Mexico was complete.

CHAPTER X

Spanish Occupation, 1598-1680

Permanent settlement and colonization now began, and, after the first year or two of comparative hardships, the Spaniards gradually spread into various sections of the Rio Grande Valley. Fortunately for the colonists, the Indians of the Tehua pueblos received them kindly, and gave material assistance in the build- of the new Spanish town. The Franciscans founded their first permanent monastery at the pueblo of San Ildefonso, near to Oñate's new city; and from that as a central point missionaries traversed the country in all directions and churches were erected in all the principal villages.

As a result of these efforts as early as 1608 no less than 8,000 Indians had been baptized; and by 1626 that number had increased to nearly 35,000. Others of the colonists, more interested in temporal things, explored the country from end to end for the precious metals. The remains of ancient workings show how enterprising were the prospectors of the eighteenth century; their labors extending from the Mexican boundary in the south to the Rio Colorado in the north.

Oñate, himself, showed great energy and ability both in the government of the colony and in his dealings with the natives.

We have already seen the untiring energy with which, in less than five months after his arrival, he made a tour of all the Pueblo provinces. The years 1599 and 1600 were occupied in exploration and in extending the settlements.

The governor then determined to attempt a more ambitious journey, and set out in June, 1601, on an expedition to the great city of the east—the famous Quivira. He took with him eighty soldiers, and was accompanied by two friars for religious duties. After the long march across the plains, he reached the object of the expedition and succeeded in making a treaty of perpetual friendship between the Quivirans and the Spaniards,

But while he was absent, many of the colonists became discouraged and even the priests lost heart, and a number deserted the infant settlement and returned to Mexico. When Oñate arrived he was greatly vexed at this and sent his nephew, Vicente

Old Church at San Juan, 1879.

de Saldivar, in hot haste to Mexico to turn back the fugitives. Don Vicente overtook the colonists and forced them to return, and then proceeded not only to Mexico, but to Spain itself, to protect the interests of his uncle.

The latter had lost none of his love of adventure, and determined to explore the unknown region to the west, if possible as far as the ocean itself. He set out on October 7, 1604, with 30 soldiers and two priests, and first visited Zuñi and then the pueblos of the Moqui province, and finally reached the Colorado river itself, which he called "Rio de Buena Esperanza" (Good Hope). Oñate was the first European to follow that great stream to its mouth, and in the course of the journey he found many different tribes of Indians. This expedition was of great importance in determining the distance of the settlements on the Rio Grande from the western shore of the continent, but it was absolutely barren of practical results. He returned by the same general route to San Gabriel, where the soldiers arrived after many privations and being reduced to the necessity of eating their horses, on April 25, 1605.

In 1605 accurred the removal of the capital from San Gabriel to Santa Fé.

Whatever was the cause of the change, time has demonstrated the wisdom of the choice; as all the experience of three hundred years has shown no locality so salubrious in its climate, and so free from the wind and storm of winter and the heat and insect pests of summer, in all the wide southwest.

For three-quarters of a century after this removal of the capital, the records that we have of the history of New Mexico are quite meagre. The growth of the colony was slow, as few cared to leave the tropical climate of Mexico to endure the privations of frontier life in the northern province, now that the romance of exploration and the hope of mineral riches was dissipated.

In 1606, we are told that a party of 800 Indians from Quivira came to Santa Fé to return the visit made by the Spaniards five years before, and brought with them to Oñate an Axtao prisoner, who was taken to Spain and presented to the king, attracting great attention wherever he journeyed.

Oñate ceased to be governor in 1608 and was succeeded by Don Pedro de Peralta. The former had encountered a series of difficulties and disappointments. The viceroy of New Spain was not always friendly, and there was frequent friction with the friars. The expense of the colonization had been enormous. The contract with the Crown, under which the expedition had been undertaken, provided for the succession of his son to his office and honors; but nothing of that kind took place, and apparently the contract was entirely abrogated.

San Juan Pueblo, Festival, 1880.

In 1617 the Cabildo of Sante Fé petitioned the king for aid for the new settlement.

In 1621, the Franciscan Missions, which claimed 16,000 converts among the Indians, were organized as the "Custodia of the Conversion of St. Paul," and Padre Alonzo Benevides came as the first custodio, bringing with him twenty-seven friars. He made a lengthy report as to the condition of New Mexico in 1626, which is altogether the best source of information as to that

Ruins of Pecos Church, 1880.

period. He tells us that at that time there were 250 Spaniards in Santa Fé, though only 50 could do military service on account of lack of arms; and there were also 700 Indians and half-breeds living there.

Two governors are mentioned during this period—Felipe

Zotylo and Manuel de Silva—of whom we know little more than the names. After them came Luis de Rosas in 1641, a governor Valdez, Alonzo Pacheco de Heredia, Fernando de Arguello in 1645, and Luis de Guzman; which brings us down to 1650.

During much of this period there was increasing friction between the civil and the religious authorities; the friars claiming almost absolute power in matters connected with the Indians, and the governors vigorously resenting this interference with their authority. Governor de Rosas was stabbed to death in 1641 or 1642 in connection with these difficulties. About this time the Inquisition was introduced, and this added to the friction. Meanwhile the Indians were becoming more and more restless under the burdens of the Spanish rule.

For a number of years after the colonization, the best of feeling existed between the native Pueblos and the newcomers, but, as time went on, the Spaniards began to assume greater powers, introduced European laws, and punished the natives for the least infraction of a foreign code of which they had never heard. The favorite penalty was slavery, as that provided the labor of which the colonists stood in need, especially in the mines, where the servitude was of the most harsh character.

Under the circumstances, the Pueblos naturally changed in their feelings from welcome and hospitality to hatred and a determination to expel the invaders whenever opportunity should be found. The middle of the seventeenth century was filled with a succession of revolts arising from this state of affairs. As one after another failed, either from lack of co-operation or because the project was divulged prematurely, the Indians learned that only by united and secret action was success to be achieved; and preparations for such an uprising were cautiously discussed at the great Pueblo festivals.

About 1645, forty Indians were hung on religious grounds and many others were flogged and imprisoned, and this brought about a revolt, which, howover, was short-lived.

Fernando de Ugarte y la Concha became governor in 1650, and shortly afterwards a plot was discovered by which the Pueblos and Apaches were to kill all of the soldiers, on the night of Holy Thursday, when all would be in church.

SPANISH OCCUPATION. 71

Shortly after this occurrence, there were risings among the Piros. In all of these cases the punishments were very severe.

In 1653, Juan de Samaniego was appointed governor, and was succeeded by Enrique de Avila y Pacheco in 1656, and he by Ber-

Interior of Pecos Church, 1880.

nardo Lopez de Mendizabal. The last named became involved in warm disputes with the officials of the Inquisition, and finally resigned in 1660. He was succeeded by Diego de Peñalosa.

Peñalosa was altogether the most picturesque character among all the New Mexican governors in the century between Oñate and De Vargas.

He was a man of fine apperance and engaging manners, very ambitious, of great assurance, and large wealth. With much energy he took up the duties of the office, visited various parts of the territory, and went as far west as Zuñi and Moqui, and planned many expeditions abroad as well as new settlements at home. But the troubles with the Inquisition were revived and for some special cause of offense, we are told that he finally arrested the commissary-general and imprisoned him for a week in the Palace. This was not forgotten nor forgiven; and when soon afterwards, he went to the City of Mexico, the high officials of the Inquisition there had him thrown into prison and subjected to a ruinous fine, and he was only set at liberty on making a public apology and humiliating act of contrition.

He again endeavored to interest the viceroy and even the king in a grand scheme of conquest, but being unsuccessful, he went to Paris and applied to the French government to take up the project, and there presented the narrative of a most remarkable expedition purporting to have been made by himself, in 1662, from Santa Fe to Quivira; the whole of which was entirely imaginative except as founded on the report of Oñate's expedition of 1601.

After Peñalosa, in 1664, came Fernando de Villanueva as governor, and he was succeeded by Juan de Medrano, Juan de Miranda, and Juan Francisco Treviño. This brings us down to 1679, when Antonio Otemin was appointed.

Meanwhile the bad feeling between the Spaniards and the Pueblos became intensified by various grievances, but especially by the severity accorded to the Indians. What they most needed was a leader of acknowledged ability, and in the excitement which followed the severe punishment of 47 Indians for alleged witchcraft, in 1675, a man came into general notice who seemed well fitted for the task. His name was Popé, of the pueblo of San Juan.

CHAPTER XI

The Pueblo Revolution

From the time that Popé became conspicuous in 1675 he seems to have been regarded as a leader, and was untiring in his endeavors to unite the whole Pueblo population in a general uprising against the Spaniards.

With this view he traveled from town to town, urging a forgetfulness of old jealousies, and using his wonderful eloquence to great effect. In this he was ably seconded by several other natives of large influence, prominent among whom were Catití, of Santo Domingo, Jaca of Taos, and Tacu of San Juan.

The day finally fixed on by the leaders for the uprising was August 10, 1680. Warned by previous failures, every means was used to secure secrecy. Not a woman was entrusted with the secret, and so intense was the feeling that Popé killed with his own hand his son-in-law Nicolas Bua, the governor of San Juan, because he was believed to be disloyal. But even all these precautions did not suffice, for on the eighth of August two Indians of Tesuque revealed the whole plot to Governor Otemin, and other Indians at San Lazaro and San Cristobal gave information to Father Bernal, the Franciscan custodio.

The fact that they were betrayed was immediately known by the Pueblo leaders, who saw that their only chance of success now lay in immediate action. Orders were consequently issued, and that very night, in all the pueblos, except those far distant, every Spaniard was slaughtered without regard to age or sex, except a few girls reserved for wives for the young braves. The news of this general massacre naturally created consternation at the capital. Otermin sent messengers through the territory directing the people at the north to concentrate at Santa Fé, and those of the south at Isleta, and immediately set about fortifying the capital.

The outlying houses were abandoned, and all the inhabitants

gathered in the plaza, the entrances to which were closed and fortified, and the palace put into condition to stand a siege.

Before the preparations were completed, the Tanos Indians were seen marching over the plains from the south. A desperate battle ensued, the Indians fighting with great energy, and the Spaniards having gradually to bring out their whole force to take part in the contest. The destruction of the natives was terrific, but by their superior numbers they were able to hold their ground until the appearance of the Tehuan army on the hills north of the city compelled Otermin to withdraw his forces within the walls and prepare for the combined attack to be expected on the morrow.

No such assault, however, took place as the Indians preferred the safer method of a regular siege. They invested the city closely on all sides and cut off the water supply, which soon produced great distress. As there was no hope of relief from without, the Spaniards finally determined to make a sortie in force; and this was gallantly executed on August 19th, the Indians being forced back with the loss of forty-seven prisoners. But even such successes were too dearly bought, and though the Spaniards executed all the prisoners in the Plaza, yet a council of war concluded that in view of the scarcity of provisions it would be better to evacuate the town. Preparations were accordingly made during the night of the 20th, and at early dawn the next morning the whole population mournfully started on their long march to the south. There were not even horses enough to carry the sick and wounded, so that the women and children as well as the men had to proceed on foot, carrying all their property and provisions in bundles on their back. Meanwhile, the Indians stolidly viewed them from the surrounding hills, making no attack, but apparently well content so long as the intruders were leaving the country.

The Spaniards continued their march down the river, hoping to find their countrymen at Isleta; but were disappointed in this, as they had already left for El Paso. The provisions were almost exhausted so that at length they were compelled to stop and send south for assistance. The call was responded to by Father Ayeta, of El Paso, who sent four wagon-loads of corn; and thus partially relieved, the fugitives continued their retreat,

THE PUEBLO REVOLUTION. 75

joining their southern brethren on the road, and finally selecting San Lorenzo twelve leagues above El Paso, as their winter quarters. Here they built rude houses, but suffered many privations from cold and hunger, and lost a large fraction of their number who sought a less unhappy life in the villages of Chihuahua.

The Spaniards who were left behind in various parts of New Mexico were, with scarcely an exception, killed after their countrymen had abandoned the country.

The Franciscan order never had suffered such a loss from the martyrdom of its members as at this time. No less than twenty-one gave up their lives on that fatal tenth of August, 1680.

Thus in the brief space of a few weeks the work of years was undone, not a Spaniard remaining in freedom in the province, and the old Pueblo authority was everywhere supreme. The new rulers were determined to obliterate every trace of the domination of their enemies. At Santa Fé the churches and monastery were burned amid the wildest acclamations. The gorgeous vestments of the priests were worn in derision by the natives and then destroyed. All the official documents and books were brought forth from the palace and burned in one vast bon-fire in the Plaza; and there also they danced the "cachina" with all the superstitious ceremonies of the old religion. Those who had been baptized were washed with amole in the Santa Fé river, in order to be cleansed from Christianity. Baptismal names were discarded, Christian marriages annulled, the mention of the names of Jesus and Mary prohibited, and estufas were everywhere substituted for the destroyed churches.

Popé, who had been the leader throughout the revolution, was now by common consent continued in authority and established himself in the palace of Santa Fé. He showed much wisdom in his public administration but gradually became more and more dictatorial until he created many enemies.

Meantime, Governor Otermin was using every endeavor to organize an expedition to reconquer the country, and, on November 5, 1681 he set out from El Paso del Norte with 146 mounted soldiers, together with all the able-bodied refugees and 112 friendly Indians, the entire party having nearly a thousand horses.

He arrived as far as Cochití, but there found the Indians in force, on the surrounding hills, under command of Catití. Meanwhile the weather had become very severe, and the provisions being nearly exhausted it was thought best to return to El Paso, where they arrived about the middle of February.

This failure on the part of Otermin seems to have led to his removal as governor, Bartolomé de Estrada Ramirez being appointed in his place in 1683. The latter did not even attempt a re-conquest, and in August of the same year was succeeded by Domingo Jironza Petriz de Cruzate, who organized several expeditions, and in 1689 penetrated as far as Zia, but did not succeed in any permanent occupation.

Thus for a number of years the country was left in the possession of its aboriginal inhabitants. They seemed to have forgotten their old wisdom and become entirely unfitted for self-government; and, instead of consolidating their power, they prepared the way by dissension and mutual destruction for an easy re-conquest by their enemies.

CHAPTER XII

The Re-Conquest

At length, in 1692, the viceroy of New Spain determined to bring about the re-occupation of New Mexico, and appointed as its governor a man of great energy, Diego de Vargas Zapata Lujan Ponce de Leon. This official immediately showed the wisdom of his choice by the promptitude of his action. Although greatly disappointed at the inadequacy of the force, he was enabled to muster, which amounted to but two hundred Spaniards and one hundred friendly Indians, yet he decided not to delay, but to strike a blow at once.

Accordingly, he left El Paso del Norte on August 21, 1692, and marched so rapidly up the Rio Grande valley that in less than twenty-three days he arrived before Santa Fé. He found the town walled and full of Indians, who had especially fortified the massive palace. The first act of the Spaniards was the important one of cutting off the water supply from the river, and then throughout the day negotiations were carried on, De Vargas using every effort to avoid a conflict. At first all overtures were unsuccessful, but finally a number of Indians came out to greet the general, and the next morning he was invited to enter the town. This he did, with Father Corvera and six unarmed soldiers and proclaimed that he had authority to pardon all past offenses if the people would now return to their allegiance. The royal banner was then unfurled and De Vargas formally took possession of the kingdom of New Mexico in the name of King Charles II.

The next important event was the submission of Luis Tupatu, who since the death of Popé had been the chief of the Pueblos. He came from San Juan and accompanied De Vargas on his marches to the other pueblos, having great influence in securing a favorable reception for the Spaniards. The effect of this signal success was quickly seen in the voluntary surrender of twelve adjacent pueblos.

Only waiting long enough to make the necessary arrangements for the new government, Vargas started on an expedition against Taos, and marched so rapidly that he arrived there on the third day from Santa Fé, and soon succeeded in inducing the Indians to return to their allegiance. This done, he returned to the capital, having been absent but eight days, and not losing a single man.

Scarcely taking time to rest, he next started, on October 17, on a very extensive expedition, which included Pecos, Santo Domingo, Cochití, Zia, Jemez and Santa Ana, at all of which places he re-established the Spanish authority. Finding much of the fall still left he concluded to visit the more distant pueblos as well; and so, starting from Santa Ana on October 30, with but eighty-nine soldiers, he marched to Isleta, Acoma, Zuñi, and even to all the Moqui towns except Oraybi.

From Zuñi, on his return, he took a short and direct route to Socorro, and from there went to El Paso, in order to collect the families that had been exiled since 1680, and the other colonists who were to settle the country. He arrived on December 20, 1692, but much delay occurred, so that it was not till October 13 of the next year that the unwieldy company, consisting of fifteen hundred persons, largely composed of women and children, with three thousand horses and mules and all the baggage of colonists commenced its march.

Vargas hoped to find the Indians as favorably disposed as when he left them, but meanwhile reports had been circulated that he was going to execute vengeance upon them, and a majority had decided to resist his approach. Lack of unity of action, howver, deprived their opposition of any great force. Santa Ana, Zia, and San Felipe gave tokens of friendly feeling, and, on December 16, 1693, the Spanish army marched into the capital without opposition, bearing the same banner which had been carried by Oñate when he entered the city almost a hundred years before.

After various ceremonies in the Plaza, the Spaniards encamped on the hills north of the city, as the palace was occupied by the Tanos Pueblos, and the houses by other Indians. The weather was unusually severe; so much so that men sent out to obtain timber to repair the church of San Miguel were obliged

THE RE-CONQUEST. 79

to return to town; and Vargas, wishing to use the public buildings for the immigrants, sent word to the Tanos Indians to return to their pueblos on the Galisteo. This order created great commotion, and the Indians concluded at a council to resist the entrance of the Spaniards.

Church of San Miguel, Santa Fe, 1880.

On December 28 they closed all the entrances to the Plaza and fortified all the ramparts. De Vargas demanded the surrender of the Indians but was only replied to by insults. An immediate assault was then made upon the town, and a fierce battle ensued throughout the entire day. Companies of Tanos and Tehua Indians came over the hills to the aid of their friends within the walls, and on the other hand the Spaniards were greatly assisted by the Indians of Pecos under their ever faithful governor, Juan Ye. The darkness of night separated the combatants, but at daybreak the Spaniards burst through the walls and captured the town with great slaughter. Many Indians escaped, but seventy. warriors, including Bolsas, the governor, were shot in the Plaza.

The capture of the capital had a great effect, but hostilities continued for over two years more, until at length the last remnants of opposition were overcome, and by the end of 1696 the whole country acknowledged the Spanish authority.

The first place repopulated, after the revolution, was Santa Cruz, to which the families that arrived from El Paso in June, 1694, were sent as soon as it was safe, in 1695.

CHAPTER XIII

The Spanish Era 1696 to 1822

Considering the brilliancy of the reconquest by Vargas it would be supposed that all would have united in sustaining his administration. But this was far from the case, and almost from the first there was friction between himself and the Cabildo which claimed to govern the capital city. His five-year term as governor expired in 1696, and Pedro Rodriguez Cubero was appointed in his place. De Vargas had applied for another term but the application arrived in Spain too late. The king, however, appreciated the value of the services of the reconquistador and promised to reappoint him when Cubero's term should expire. Cubero arrived and commenced his administration July 2, 1697. He ordered the arrest of Vargas and treated him with great harshness, imposing a heavy fine and keeping him in close confinement until July, 1700, when he immediately left for Mexico to seek redress.

In 1699, Governor Cubero made a tour of the rest of the territory, receiving the submission of Acoma, of Laguna (then newly established), and of Zuñi; and carrying on active negotiations for the Christianizing of the Moquis. But soon after Zuñi itself was abandoned both by the friar resident there and the military.

In 1703 De Vargas, who had been reappointed governor, reappeared, Cubero having left without waiting to meet him. The reconquistador had meanwhile received from the king the title of Marquez de la Nava de Brazinas, and reassumed office in Santa Fé on November 10, with his friend Juan Paez Hurtado, as lieutenant-governor. He had many plans for the firmer establishment of Spanish authority, but these were all cut short by his sudden death while on an expedition against the Navajos at Bernalillo, on April 14, 1704. His remains were interred behind the altar of the Church of St. Francis, now the Cathedral, at Santa Fe, where his monument still exists.

Hurtado succeeded as acting-governor, and served till March 10, 1705, when a governor *ad interim*, appointed by the viceroy of New Spain, arrived, in the person of Francisco Cuervo y Valdez. But the king of Spain had his own friends to favor, and appointed Jose Chacon Medina Salazar y Villaseñor, Marquez

The Marquis de la Peñuela Autograph and Rubric.

de la Peñuela, to succeed De Vargas, when news of the death of the latter reached Spain.

Meanwhile, in 1706, Governor Cuervo founded the Villa of Albuquerque, which he named in honor of the viceroy of New

Spain, who had given him his appointment; and established thirty families there.

The Marquez de la Peñuela is known to all New Mexicans and multitudes of tourists, from the inscription on the ancient beam which forms a part of the ceiling of the historic church of San Miguel in Santa Fé. This reads as follows:"El Señor Marquez de la Peñuela hizo esta fabrica; el Alferes Real Don Agustin Flores Vergara su criado. Ano de 1710."—"His Lordship, the Marquis de la Peñuela, erected this building; the Royal Ensign Don Agustin Flores Vergara, his servant. A. D. 1710."

It was the custom among Spaniards at this period, and long afterward, to attach to the signature a flourish, called "rubrica," which became as much a representative of the individual using it as the signature itself. In some cases the rubrica was used instead of the full signature. Many of these rubricas are very elaborate and show great ingenuity. The one which was used by Governor Peñuela is very remarkable and is therefore reproduced here. It is taken from a document dated January 29, 1712, in the possession of the Author.

Peñuela was succeeded by Juan Ignacio Flores Mogollon, who assumed the office October 5, 1712, and continued as governor for exactly three years, to a day. He was born in Seville, had been governor of Nuevo Leon, and was a man of experience, but was now quite old and infirm. He is commemorated by the Mogollon Mountains in southwest New Mexico. He was relieved on October 5, 1715, and the viceroy appointed Felix Martinez as acting-governor until a regular appointment should be made by the king. Martinez was a man of violent temper and was accused of unblushing corruption in office, even to the extent of dividing all the Indian captives taken in a fight with the Utes and Comanches with his brother, and having them sold on joint account in New Biscay. The viceroy became dissatisfied with his conduct, and in September, 1716, ordered him to report in Mexico, and directed Captain Antonio Valverde v Cosio, who was in command at El Paso, to proceed to Santa Fé and become acting-governor.

Through all this period there was the same succession of border troubles, of incursions by wild Indians against both Spaniards and Pueblos, and of return expeditions by the latter against the savages.

The next regular governor was Juan Domingo de Bustamante, who held office for two terms of five years each, assuming the position March 2, 1722.

The successor of Bustamante was Gervasio Cruzat y Gongora, in office from 1731 to 1736, and he was succeeded in the latter year by Enrique de Olavide y Michelena, named temporarily by the viceroy, who served until the regular governor appointed by the king, Gaspar Domingo de Mendoza, arrized in 1739. During his administration the number of Spanish inhabitants, not including soldiers and their families, was found to be 9,747, residing in 24 towns.

The next governor was Joaquin Codallos y Rabal, a major of the Spanish army, who held the office from 1743 to 1749, and was succeeded by Tomas Velez Cachupin in May, 1749. During the administration of Governor Codallos, in 1748, the pueblo of Sandia was re-established by Padre Menchero, a zealous Franciscan, who collected a large number of Tihua Indians, rescued from Moqui, and settled them on the Rio Grande. Wars with the Utes and Comanches were almost as regular as the seasons, but with varying results. In October, 1747, Governor Codallos overtook a large body of them above Abiquiu, killed 107, captured 206, and secured about 1,000 horses. In 1751 Governor Cachupin almost equaled this achievement by killing 101, and capturing the remaining 44, of a band of Comanches who had made a raid on Galisteo; and only lost one of his own 164 men.

In 1754, Governor Cachupin was succeeded by Francisco Antonio Maria del Valle, whose memory is preserved at Santa Fé by the gift made by himself and his wife to the Church of Our Lady of Light on the Plaza, of a carved stone reredos, which is now to be seen back of the altar in the cathedral. The church was his own gift to the soldiers of the garrison and hence was called the "Castrense," or military chapel; and remained until exchanged by Bishop Lamy for other property.

Governor Del Valle held office till late in 1760, and then Mateo Antonio de Mendoza acted for a few months, and was succeeded in 1761 by Manuel Portillo Urrisola for another short period; after which, on February 1, 1762, Governor Cachupin, who had been re-appointed by the king, again took possession of the office. During this second term of Cachupin the first expedition into what is now Colorado was made in search of mineral wealth. The exploring party was in charge of Juan Maria Rivera, and penetrated the San Juan country and the region of the Gunnison and Uncompagre, where they discovered considerable silver and consequently named the mountain and the river La Plata.

After Governor Cachupin, in 1767, came Pedro Fermin de Mendinueta, as governor and captain-general; and he was the last of the Spanish officials to hold this latter title. At this time the number of Spanish soldiers stationed in the territory was only eighty, who had headquarters at Santa Fé; and the governor reported that besides the troops located there, there were about 200 men among the colonists capable of military service, but very poorly supplied with arms. Many explorations were made about this time, mostly in the direction of the Pacific. In 1774, Captain Juan Bautista de Anza headed an expedition to the west which succeeded in reaching the Spanish settlements in California by way of the Gila. In 1776, Padre Escalante attempted to reach the Pacific by a northern route and penetrated as far as Utah Lake, when he was compelled to return by way of Moqui; and about the same time Padre Francisco Garces made his memorable trip along the valley of the Colorado and through parts of California and Arizona.

Governor Mendinueta continued in office until March, 1778, when Francisco Trebol Navarro, who for a number of years had been alcalde mayor of the Albuquerque district, was acting-governor for a short time; and toward the end of the year, Ansa, now a lieutenant-colonel, was appointed governor. He was a native of Sonora, familiar with the country and people, and made an excellent official. He carried on a vigorous warfare against the Comanches, especially in 1779, when he made a rapid march to the northeast with about 1,000 men, and killed Cuerno Verde, the Comanche chieftain, as well as securing a great victory over the tribe.

In 1789, Fernando de la Concha came as governor; and in turn he was succeeded, in 1794, by Fernando Chacon, who was still in office at the end of the century. At this time and down to the beginning of the traffic over the Santa Fé trail we are told that there was no money in New Mexico, but all business transacted was by exchange of land or animals or commodities. There was a great fair every year at Taos in mid-summer, when the wild tribes came in from the plains, with skins, principally of buffalo and deer, buffalo meat, etc., for exchange for iron implements, beads, and various manufactured articles. In January occurred the annual fair at Chihuahua, which was attended by the people of all the northern provinces, and to which the New Mexicans went in long caravans for protection while passing through deserts like the Jornada del Muerto. These caravans sometimes included no less than 500 persons, and their departure and arrival were the great events of the year. The merchants at Chihuahua became rich through this trade, and the traders in their turn made very large profits from the Spanish settlers and the Indians. An instance is given of the purchase in Chihuahua of a Guacamaya, a parrot of gay plumage, for eight dollars, and the sale of the feathers in New Mexico for $492. This trade continued to be all of the commercial business of the country until the opening of the Santa Fé Trail.

In the spring of 1805, Colonal Joaquin del Real Alencaster came to succeed Governor Chacon, who had served two terms of five years each. In 1806, owing to the purchase of Louisiana by the United States three years before, Lieutenant Melgares was sent from Chihuahua with 100 dragoons on an expedition along the border to explore the country and conciliate the Indians. He followed the Red river into the present Oklahoma, visited the Pawnee nation in Kansas, distributed Spanish flags and medals, and then returned to Santa Fé in October.

The first arrivals across the plains from the Mississippi Valley occurred in 1804 and 1805, when La Lande and Pursley appeared in Santa Fé; and on March 3, 1807, Lieutenant Pike and his little company were brought into the city from the north. These events will be treated of in separate chapters; Pike's exploits in Chapter XIV, and the Santa Fé Trail in Chapter XVII.

The next regular governor was Jose Manrique, who was governor or governor *ad interim* from 1808 to 1814, and again for a short time in 1819.

During the term of Governor Manrique occurred the election of the only representative which New Mexico ever had in the Spanish Cortes. There were three leading candidates for this distinguished position, Antonio Ortiz, Juan Rafael Ortiz, and Pedro Bautista Pino, and the latter was chosen. He proceeded to take the long journey by the way of Mexico and Vera Cruz to Spain, where the regular Spanish government was then in session at Cadiz. While residing in Spain he published a *Report,* descriptive of New Mexico, its people, and government, which is one of the most valuable documents connected with New Mexican history. A copy of this interesting work is in the library of the Historical Society.

Alberto Maynez was the next executive, with the title of civil and military governor. He served in 1814 and 1815, and again in 1817.

Pedro Maria de Allande succeeded to the title in 1816, and again in 1818, after the second period of Maynez's authority.

Facundo Melgares was the last of the Spanish governors, the revolution of 1821 being successful in establishing Mexican independence. It was Governor Melgares who commanded the expedition into the Indian Territory in 1806, and subsequently had charge of the escort of Pike to Chihuahua, in 1807.

Melgares was a man of distinguished family, liberal education, immense fortune and great military ability. The long line of Spanish governors, beginning with Oñate, and containing many distinguished names, finds a fitting termination in the person of Melgares, of whom history speaks only in terms of praise.

CHAPTER XIV

The Expedition of Lieutenant Pike—1806-7

Shortly after the acquisition of the vast territory then called Louisiana, from the French by the United States, the government of the latter undertook the exploration of this immense domain. Captains Lewis and Clark were selected by the president to explore the then unvisited sources of the Missouri, and Lieutenant Zebulon Montgomery Pike to follow the Mississippi to its source. The expedition of Lieutenant Pike occupied nearly nine months, extending to the last day of April, 1806, when he returned.

Soon after his arrival he was requested by General Wilkinson to take command of another expedition then being fitted out at St. Louis, the primary object of which was to conduct a number of Osage Indian captives up the Missouri and Osage rivers to the Indian town of Grand Osage. The instructions then provided that Lieutenant Pike should endeavor to bring about a permanent peace between the Kansas and Osage nations; "establish a good understanding with the Yanctons, Tetaus, or Comanches," and finally "to ascertain the direction, extent, and navigation of the Arkansaw and Red rivers." As to the possibility of meeting inhabitants of New Mexico, the instructions of the general were as follows:

"As your interview with the Comanches will probably lead you to the head branches of the Arkansaw and Red rivers, you may find yourself approximated to the settlements of New Mexico, and there it will be necessary you should move with great circumspection to keep clear of any hunting or reconnoitering parties from that province and to prevent alarm or offense."

This expedition started from the landing at Belle Fontaine on July 15, 1806—the party consisting of two lieutenants, one surgeon, one sergeant, two corporals, sixteen privates, and one interpreter. The surgeon was Dr. Robinson, who was a volunteer, giving his services as compensation for transportation. From August 20th to September 1st, Lieutenant Pike remained at Grand Osage, holding councils with the chiefs of the Osage nation, and on September 29th he held a grand council with the Pawnees at their principal village, not less than 400 warriors being present.

At this point he saw evidences of the Spanish expedition under Melgares which had recently visited there from New Mexico. This expedition consisted of 100 dragoons of the regular army drawn from Chihuahua, and 500 mounted militia of New Mexico, all equipped with ammunition for six months. They descended the Red river 233 leagues, held councils there with the chief of the Tetaus, and afterwards struck off northeast to the Pawnee nation, where they held a grand council, presented Spanish flags and medals, and also a commission to Characterish, the head chief, from the governor of New Mexico.

After leaving the Pawnee capital, Lieutenant Pike proceeded westerly between the Arkansas and the Kansas rivers, seeing many prairie-dogs, which he calls *Wishtonwishes* from the sound of their cry, and of which he tells us almost the exact story afterwards repeated by Horace Greeley of their living in the same hole with a rattlesnake, a horned toad, and a land tortoise. On the 28th of October, he detached Lieutenant Wilkinson with five soldiers to make a trip down the Arkansas river in canoes, for the purpose of exploring its whole course to the Mississippi. On the 15th of November he came in sight of the Rocky Mountains, and soon after encountered almost constant snows, suffering great hardships—as the company had only summer cotton clothes—and on the 3d of December reached the great mountain which bears his name—"Pike's Peak;" and he says that in all the wanderings of the party for over two months, it was never out of their sight.

The hardships endured during this period are almost beyond description; the feet of the men became frosted so that they could only proceed with the utmost pain, and finally several had to be left in sheltered localities, and supplied with food by the remainder. The party subsisted entirely on the product of the chase, and sometimes for three full days were without a mouthful to eat. In December the expedition determined to leave the valley of the Arkansas and proceed southerly, to strike the headwaters of the Red river, which they expected to find at that point; each of the party, including the commander himself and Dr. Robinson, carrying forty-five pounds of baggage, besides provisions and arms, making an aggregate of seventy pounds burden. At length, on the 30th of January, they arrived on the banks of a stream which they believed to be the long-looked-for Red river. Here they concluded to build a stockade, where four or five might defend themselves while the others went back to carry assistance to the poor fellows who had necessarily been left at various points, the intention being, when all should be assembled, to proceed down the Red river to Natchitoches, then the most westerly post in southern Louisiana. At this point Dr. Robinson, who had business in New Mexico, left the party in order to proceed to Santa Fé, which they calculated was then nearer than it would be from any other point.

While most of the men were absent, and the remainder were at work building the fort, Pike himself usually employed himself in hunting; and on February 15, he discovered two horsemen who proved to be a Spanish dragoon and a Pueblo Indian, both well armed. They seemed surprised at the appearance of the fort, but Pike informed them of his intention of going down the river to Natchitoches as soon as his party was prepared. The two visitors stated that they could reach Santa Fé in two days, but never intimated that Pike was wrong in supposing himself on the banks of the Red river. Gradually the frozen men who had been left behind were brought in—with the exception of two still unable to walk. Of them Pike says, "they sent me some of the bones taken out of their feet, and conjured me by all that was sacred not to leave them to perish far from the civilized world."

On the 26th of February the report of the guard's gun announced the appearance of strangers, and soon after two Frenchmen arrived. These informed Pike that Governor Alencaster, of New Mexico, had heard that the Ute Indians were about to attack the little expedition, and therefore had sent an officer with fifty dragoons to protect them. Scarcely had this notification been received, when the Spanish party came in sight, consisting not only of the fifty dragoons but also fifty mounted militia of the province. The officers in command of the Spanish expedition were Ygnacio Saltelo and Bartolomé Fernandez, both lieutenants. They said that the governor, having learned that Pike's party had lost its route, had sent them to offer assistance to reach the Red river, the nearest navigable point of which was eight days' journey from Santa Fé. "What," said Pike, interrupting him, "is not this the Red river?" Imagine his amazement at the answer, "No, sir! it is the Rio del Norte." These words showed that he had unwittingly passed the frontiers of the United States, and actually erected a fort on Spanish soil, within the borders of New Mexico. His first act, on receiving this astonishing information, was to order his men to take down the American flag, which had been hoisted over the works. The Spanish commander then said that the governor was anxious to see them at Santa Fé as soon as possible, and had provided 100 horses and mules to take the party and their baggage to the capital. Pike at first refused to go until the detachment which he sent under a sergeant to bring in the two men still absent had returned; but it was finally arranged that he should proceed with one of the lieutenants and half the Spanish force, leaving two men to meet the sergeant's party on their return.

On the journey to Santa Fé the first town of importance which they saw, after a march of a little more than 100 miles, was Ojo Caliente. Here they found the first real Mexican houses which they had seen, and Pike describes at some length the flat roofs, water-spouts, narrow doors, and small windows—some with mica lights. The next day they marched down Ojo Caliente river to its junction with the Chama, observing on the way the ruins of ancient pueblo towns, as well as several little inhabited villages, all of which had round towers to defend the inhabitants from Indian incursions. Here they experienced the characteristic hospitality of the Mexican people; who invited them into their houses, dressed the feet of the young men who had been frozen— and in short, to use the language of Pike, "brought to my recollection the hospitality of the ancient patriarchs, and caused me to sigh with regret at the corruption of that noble principle by the polish of modern ages."

The same day they continued down the Chama to the Rio Grande and across to the pueblo of San Juan, where all the officers and men were hospitably treated. The next morning they marched through Santa Cruz and San Ildefonso to Tesuque, where they changed horses and prepared for their entry into the capital and appearance before the governor. The condition of Pike's party as to clothing was so lamentable as to be almost ludicrous. When they left their horses on the Arkansas, all articles were abandoned that were not essential to safety. So on arriving at Santa Fé the commander was dressed in blue trousers, moccasins, blanket, coat, and a cap made of scarlet cloth lined with fur skin; and the men, in leggings, breechcloths, and leather coats—and not a hat in the whole company. In such garb they did not make a very imposing appearance.

They had left the fort on the Conejos, February 26, and arrived at Santa Fé on the evening of Tuesday, March 3.

On entering the city, Lieutenant Pike was conducted to the palace, where he says:

"We were ushered in through various rooms, the floors of which were covered with skins of buffalo, bear, or some other animal. We waited in a chamber for some time until his excellency appeared, when we arose, and the following conversation took place in French:

"Gov. Do you speak French?
"Pike. Yes, sir.
"Gov. You come to reconnoitre our country, do you?
"Pike. I march to reconnoitre our own.
"Gov. In what character are you?
"Pike. In my proper character, an officer of the United States Army.
"Gov. How many men have you?
"Pike. Fifteen.
"Gov. When did you leave St. Louis?
"Pike. 15th of July.
"Gov. Well, return with Mr. Bartholomew to his house, and come here again at seven o'clock, and bring your papers.

At the hour appointed we returned, when the governor demanded my papers. I told him I understood my trunk was taken possession of by his guard. He expressed his surprise, and immediately ordered it in.

"He then requested to see my commission and orders, which I

read to him in French; on which he got up and gave me his hand for the first time, and said he was happy to be acquainted with me as a man of honor and a gentleman; that I could retire this evening and take my trunk with me; that on the morrow he would make further arrangements."

The next day, after examining the contents of Pike's trunk, the governor informed him that he must go with his men to Chihuahua, to appear before the commandant-general. The following conversation then ensued, which Pike has preserved in full in his journal:

"Pike. If we go to Chihuahua, we must be considered as prisoners of war.

"Gov. By no means.

"Pike. But, sir, I cannot consent to be led 300 or 400 leagues out of my route without its being by force of arms.

"Gov. I know you do not go voluntarily, but I will give you a certificate from under my hand of my having obliged you to march. You will dine with me to-day, and march afterwards to a village about six miles distant, where the remainder of your escort is waiting for you, under the command of the officer who commanded the expedition to the Pawnees."

After the dinner, the governor drove Pike, D'Almansa, and Mr. Bartholomew, who had proved a special friend to the Americans, three miles on the road to the south, the coach being attended by a guard of cavalry; and on parting said to his prisoner-guest: "Remember Alencaster in peace or war."

Accompanied by Bartholomew and the guard, Pike continued on through a blinding sand, and passed the night at the priest's house, at La Bajada. Shortly after noon of the next day they arrived at the pueblo of Santo Domingo, where the insignia of the governor appears to have been nearly the same as at present, as he was distinguished by "a cane with a silver head and black tassel."

On Friday, March 6, they arrived at San Felipe, where they crossed the Rio Grande on a bridge of eight arches, which seems to have attracted Pike's attention specially, as he gives a full description of its construction. Here they stopped at the house of the padre, Father Rubi, whose hospitality made the stay a pleasant one, and at Albuquerque they were similarly entertained by Father Ambrosio Guerra.

A short distance further south Pike was rejoiced to meet Dr. Robinson, who was being conveyed to Chihuahua by Don Facundo Melgares, who was now to assume command of the guard that was conducting Pike. This Melgares was the same who had commanded the Pawnee expedition, and was described by Robinson to Pike in the highest terms as a gentleman and soldier.

On the 21st of March the whole party arrived at El Paso, and on April 2 reached Chihuahua, where Pike immediately had an audience with the general commanding, Don Nemecio Salcedo, who took his papers for examination, and also requested him to write a brief sketch of his travels on this expedition.

After being detained for some time, which, however, was spent quite pleasantly, owing to the hospitality of many of the leading citizens, Pike and Robinson were sent by a route nearly directly eastward, toward Natchitoches, which was the nearest United States post.

On the 1st of July, 1807—but three weeks short of a year from the time of his departure from St. Louis—after crossing the whole of what is now the state of Texas, Pike entered the town of Natchitoches with Dr. Robinson. "Language," says he, "cannot express the gaiety of my heart when I once more beheld the standard of my country waved aloft. 'All hail,' cried I, 'the ever-sacred name of *country*, in which is embraced that of kindred, friends, and every other tie which is dear to the soul of man!' "

CHAPTER XV

Mexican Government, 1821-46

The patriotic sentiment for Mexican independence which had never been quenched from the time of the first revolution under Hidalgo in 1810, assumed practical form in 1821 by the Plan of Iguala, which may be called the Mexican Declaration of Independence, promulgated on February 24.

The revolution was so successful that on August 24 a treaty was signed by the viceroy recognizing the independence of Mex,- ico. As the Spanish commander of the City of Mexico refused to surrender that city, it was captured by General Iturbide on September 27, and Spanish authority was at an end in New Spain.

This change in the government necessarily affected New Mexico, but there were no conflicts there, the almost isolated territory simply accepting the new conditions as they came.

There was a burst of enthusiasm in Santa Fé over the achievement of Mexican independence. When the news arrived on the day after Christmas, 1821, that Iturbide had captured the city of Mexico there was great excitement, Governor Melgares made an inspiring address to a great meeting in the Plaza, and it was determined to have a grand demonstration in honor of Mexican independence on January 6. Then there were decorations and salutes, and processions and illuminations, day and night. The alcalde, Pédro Armendaris, led a grand march. A patriotic drama was presented, in which Santiago Abreu represented Independence, Vicar Terrasas personated Religion; and Chaplain Osio, the Union. Thus the new independence was received with loud acclaim.

RULERS

ANTONIO VISCARRA was the first regular executive under Mexican authority. The title was now changed from Governor to

"Political Chief." Governor Viscarra succeeded Melgares on July 5, 1822, and was also acting governor in 1828.

He was succeeded in June, 1823, by Francisco Xavier Chaves, a prominent native New Mexican, who acted for a few weeks until the regular appointment of

BARTOLOME BACA, who was in authority during half of 1823, and until September 13, 1825, when he was succeeded by—

ANTONIO NARBONA, who held the office until May 20, 1827. He was a Canadian.

MANUEL ARMIJO then obtained the position, holding it at this time but about a year, when—

JOSE ANTONIO CHAVES succeeded, and held the office for three years.

SANTIAGO ABREU became Political Chief in 1831, and continued until some time in 1832. He and his two brothers, Ramon and Marcelino, all came from Mexico some time before, and all were killed in the revolution of 1837.

FRANCISCO SARRACINO was Political Chief, 1833 to May 14, 1835, except in October, 1834, when Juan Rafael Ortiz was acting executive.

In May, 1835, Mariano Chaves became acting Jefe Politico for three months, until the arrival from Mexico, in July, 1835, of—

ALBINO PEREZ, who served as Political Chief until the new Mexican constitution went into effect and New Mexico was changed from a territory into a department, and its executive from a Political Chief to a Governor. The new arrangement went into operation in May, 1837, Perez being the first governor, and holding the position until he was murdered in the revolution of that year. During the insurrection, and while José Gonzales was claiming to be governor, the legitimate authority was held by—

PEDRO MUNOZ, a colonel in the army, as acting governor, until the executive power was assumed by—

MANUEL ARMIJO, first as commanding general, and after the execution of Gonzales in January, 1838, as governor. He was soon after regularly appointed to the latter office, and held it until suspended by the inspector general. For a brief time in 1841—

MEXICAN GOVERNMENT. 97

ANTONIO SANDOVAL appears as acting governor; and during the suspension of Armijo—
MARIANO MARTINEZ DE LEJANZA was governor for some time in 1844 to September 18, 1845, and—

Governor Armijo.

JOSE CHAVES from the latter date to December, when Armijo was returned to the executive office, and again assumed its duties.

MANUEL ARMIJO was the last Mexican governor, holding the position until the American occupation.

JUAN BAUTISTA VIGIL Y ALARID became acting governor for a short time after Armijo's retreat, and as such delivered the capital to General Kearny, August 18, 1846.

All through this period, down to the final overthrow of the Navajos long after the American occupation, there existed an almost constant condition of warfare with that powerful tribe. They made frequent incursions into the settlements—much as the Comanches did in the preceding century; and in turn armed expeditions were made into their country, with a view to their punishment and the destruction of their villages and property.

In 1824, Durango, Chihuahua, and New Mexico were united to constitute a state of the Mexican Union; but this arrangement did not last for any great length of time.

In 1828 the Mexican congress passed a law expelling all native-born Spaniards (called Cachupines) from the republic. This, of course, affected a number in New Mexico, including the Franciscan friars, who were all forced to leave, with the exception of two, named Albino and Castro.

In 1833, Bishop Zubiría, of Durango, made a visitation throughout New Mexico, and was received with great enthusiasm. He made quite a protracted stay in Santa Fé, and visited a number of towns in the territory. Bishop Zubiría made another visitation to New Mexico in 1845, and again in 1850.

In 1835 the first newspaper enterprise was attempted, as will appear in Chapter XXII.

In 1837 occurred the alteration in the general system of government throughout the republic, which changed New Mexico from a territory into a department, and by its unpopular features led to an insurrection of such importance that it has appeared best to treat it briefly in a separate chapter. (See Chapter XVI.)

Since the first passage across the plains in the early part of the century, the traffic with the United States had been steadily increasing, until it had grown to very large proportions. The general interest in the Santa Fé Trail, has caused that subject also to have a separate chapter devoted to it. (See Chapter XVII.)

Pioneers

This intercourse between the valleys of the Mississippi and the Rio Grande, naturally brought into New Mexico merchants and traders from the east, and they, together with trappers and hunters who settled down near the scenes of their active life, constituted a population now generally known as the "Pioneers," or the "Old Timers." Many of them were of the parentage known as "St. Louis French;" and hence come the French names which exist throughout the north of the territory.

Among the first thus to establish a business was Antonio Roubidoux, who settled at Taos in 1822. Charles Beaubien came to the same town in 1827, and a year later married the sister of Don Pedro Valdez. He was one of the grantees of the enormous "Beaubien and Miranda Grant," to which his son-in-law gave the name of the "Maxwell Grant."

Ceran St. Vrain, one of the most celebrated of southwestern pioneers, lived for many years at Taos, and subsequently at Mora, where his grave now is. The Bents built "Bent's Fort" in 1829, and in 1832 Bent and St. Vrain commenced business at Taos. There Charles Bent married, and lived until his appointment as governor, and violent death in 1847. Kit Carson first came from Missouri to Santa Fé in 1826; afterwards going to Taos, where he studied Spanish with Kinkead, and through all of his after life, retained that as his home. Maxwell, on his "Home Ranch" on the Cimarron, lived like a feudal chief, dispensing a lavish hospitality, and literally "lord of all he surveyed." The oldest living "American" in Santa Fé for many years was James Conklin, who came in 1825, and died in June, 1883. Samuel B. Watrous, the father of the town of that name, arrived in 1835, and for a considerable time lived at the Placers. James Bonney, whose hospitality both Emory and Abert record, was the original settler at La Junta (Watrous), in 1842, his house being the first one seen in 1846 for a distance of 775 miles in coming from the east. Peter Joseph, a native of the Azores, came to Taos in 1844, and established himself in business.

Texan Santa Fe Expedition

In the year 1841 great excitement was produced by reports of the coming of an invading army from Texas, for the purpose of conquering the territory. George W. Kendall, the editor of the New Orleans *Picayune,* who accompanied this expedition simply as a traveler, says that it had no intention of making war, but only to endeavor to open a mercantile trade. The Mexican authorities, however, regarded it as a direct invasion of their territory, and terrible stories were circulated as to the ferocity of the Texans, who, it was said, would burn, slay, and destroy wherever they went.

The expedition set out from Austin on the 18th of June, 1841, under command of General McLeod; and consisted of 270 mounted volunteers and about fifty others, including commissioners, merchants, etc. Their march was a very arduous one, as it passed through a country entirely untraveled. When a long distance out on the plains, Lieutenant Hull and four men were killed by the Caygua Indians; and all suffered greatly on account of the difficulty in finding water. They ultimately reached the frontier settlements of New Mexico, near Fort Bascom, and soon after met Mexican troops, commanded by Damasio Salazar. After various experiences they were all taken prisoners by combined deceit and force, and narrowly escaped being shot by order of Salazar, through the intervention of Don Gregorio Vigil. They were marched to San Miguel and imprisoned there, but received much sympathy from the women all along the route.

On the 17th of October the whole Texan expedition marched out of San Miguel, on the way to the city of Mexico, under a strong guard commanded by Damasio Salazar. The story of their sufferings and privations, of the numberless cruelties and persecutions inflicted by Salazar; of the great contrast in their treatment when they were transferred at El Paso to the care of General J. M. Elias Gonzales, who put Salazar under arrest; of the kindness and hospitality of this General "Elias" and Padre Ortiz, and of their long imprisonment in Mexico—is graphically told by Mr. Kendall in his book entitled "The Santa Fé Expedition."

In 1844 Governor Martinez issued a proclamation which contains the last arrangement of civil divisions under the Mexican rule, and also gives the estimated populations. The districts are as follows:

MEXICAN GOVERNMENT. 101

North District—Counties of Rio Arriba and Taos, with populations of 15,000 and 14,200.

Central District—Counties of Santa Fé, Santa Ana, and San Miguel del Bado, with populations of 12,500, 10,500, and 18,800.

South District—Counties of Valencia and Bernalillo. Populations 20,000 and 8,204.

This makes the total population of the territory 99,204.

Governor Martinez was a special friend of education. He sent a number of the most promising young men in the territory to Durango and the city of Mexico to receive military educations; and established additional government schools in Santa Fé.

Mariano Martinez was the only governor except Perez sent direct from Mexico itself. He was a distinguished military man, of fine appearance and progressive ideas. It was he who planted the first trees in the Plaza of Santa Fé, which had before been a sandy waste. He also made a park in front of the Rosario chapel, and an avenue of trees leading to it. For lack of care, all of those trees perished. Governor Martinez is also remembered on account of the killing of the Ute chief, Panasiyave, with a blow from his chair, in the reception room of the palace, when he was attacked by six chiefs who were dissatisfied with the presents given to them. This was on September 7, 1844.

During the Mexican régime New Mexico was from time to time represented in the Mexican congress. Among the most distinguished representatives were Antonio José Martinez, of Taos, Juan Felipe Ortiz, of Santa Fé, and Diego Archuleta, of Rio Arriba.

GOLD MINING

In 1828 occurred the first discovery of gold, at the Old Placers, since known as Dolores. Placer mining was carried on successfully here for a number of years, although the methods employed were very primitive and the lack of water a great drawback. Most of the work was done in the winter when water could be obtained by melting snow. From 1832 to 1835 the annual product of these placers was $60,000 to $80,000, decreasing slightly thereafter. Occasionally large nuggets were found, the largest being worth $3,400.

In 1839 the "New Placers" were discovered, where the town of Golden now is. It was then called Tuerto, and quickly grew to importance. In 1845 there were twenty-two stores there, and the business was greater than that of Santa Fé. As many as 2,000 men congregated there in the winter, and the annual output for several years was over $200,000. This diminished gradually, as the richest gravel was worked out, until both Old and New Placers were practically deserted.

CHAPTER XVI

The Insurrection of 1837

To understand the causes which led to this outbreak, we must go back two years, to the time when Albino Perez, a colonel of the Mexican army, was appointed Political Chief by President Santa Ana, in 1835. Almost ever since the independence of Mexico the people of the territory had been governed by native New Mexicans; but Governor Perez was an entire stranger, sent from Mexico; and even if he had been absolutely perfect, his appointment would have occasioned discontent. The feeling was increased when, in April, 1837, the new Mexican constitution went into effect, which changed the territory into a department and imposed taxes to which the people had never before been subject. The opponents of the government exaggerated the bad features of the new system so as to render them still more obnoxious, until the people raised the standard of revolution. This was on the first of August, 1837. Santa Cruz became the headquarters of the movement, and within two days a large number of men dissatisfied with the government had collected there, embracing many Mexicans from the northern counties, and the majority of the Pueblo Indians from the adjacent villages, except San Juan.

As soon as Governor Perez received news of this revolt, he assembled what troops he had at command, and called on the militia to report for duty, but to this call received a very lukewarm response. The Indians of San Juan and Santo Domingo, however, remained apparently true, and accompanied ·by the warriors from those pueblos and his own soldiers, he marched to put down the rebels. These he met on the second day, near San Yldefonso, but upon approaching them, nearly all of the governor's army deserted, leaving so few faithful that he was forced to move with all speed toward Santa Fé. Finding that there was no security at the palace, the governor left the city at 10 o'clock at night to escape to the south, but the roads were all blocked by revolutionists, and his party was soon forced to retreat again towards the capital. Traveling on foot, the better to conceal his identity, Governor Perez reached the house of Salvador Martinez, about a league southwest of Santa Fé, and took refuge there, but was soon found by Indians from Santo Domingo and almost instantly killed. The exact place of his assassination is now marked by a stone monument, erected in 1901 by the Daughters of the American Revolution. With savage cruelty they cut off his head and carried it to the headquarters of the insurgents, near the Rosario church, in the western outskirts of Santa Fé. On the same day Jesus Maria Alarid, secretary of state, Santiago Abreu, formerly governor, Ramon Abreu and Marcelino Abreu, brothers of the ex-governor, and others, were overtaken on the road and killed.

All this was on the 9th of August; and the next day the insurgents entered the city without opposition and José Gonzales, of Taos, was elected governor, and duly installed in office in the palace.

On August 27 and 28 a general assembly composed of the influential citizens in the northern half of the territory, met at Santa Fé, at the palace, and ratified the acts of the revolutionists. Among those participating was Manuel Armijo, but almost immediately thereafter he left for the Rio Abajo or lower country, where he organized a counter-revolution and prepared to march to Santa Fé with a considerable force.

The sentiment against the revolutionists was formulated in what is known as the "Pronunciamiento de Tomé," promulgated on September 8, 1837. This declared that until other orders they would recognize the prefect of the district of Albuquerque as tthe legal authority in New Mexico; that an army be raised to be commanded by Manuel Armijo, with Mariano Chaves as second in command, and was signed by Manuel Armijo, Francisco Ignacio Madariaga (the parish priest of Tomé), José Salazar, Pablo Salazar, José Francisco Montoya, and Miguel de Olona.

When Gonzales heard that Armijo was marching up from Albuquerque, he withdrew from the capital to Santa Cruz, which was the center of the revolutionary feeling. Armijo thereupon

THE INSURRECTION OF 1837.

entered Santa Fé and proclaimed himself commander-general of the province. He immediately sent dispatches to the central government in Mexico, stating that he had overthrown the rebellion; and as a result was appointed governor of New Mexico—a position which he held for the greater part of nine years. Armijo made a rapid march to Santa Cruz in January, 1838, and succeeded in defeating tthe entire rebel army and capturing all the leaders. Immediate punishment followed, no mercy being shown. On January 24 the two brothers Montoya, Juan José Esquibel, and Juan Vigil were executed near the Garita in the northern part of Santa Fé. Gonzales was killed by the immediate command of Armijo himself directly after the victory of La Cañada. The story is that Gonzales, on being captured, was brought before Armijo, and on seeing the general, Gonzales came forward with hand extended, saying, "How do you do, Compañero?" as was proper between two of equal rank as governors. Armijo replied, "How do you do, Compañero? Confess yourself, Compañero." Then turning to his soldiers, added, "Now shoot my compañero!"—which command was immediately executed. This effectually ended the revolution of 1837.

CHAPTER XVII

The Santa Fé Trail

Mexico was settled early in the sixteenth century, and the Spaniards soon after penetrated over 1,500 miles to the north and occupied the valley of the Rio Grande, and another colonization from England and France populated the eastern shores of what is now the United States and Canada early in the seventeenth century, and extended westward to the Mississippi Valley; yet it was left for the nineteenth century to see any communication whatever between these two populations, situated on the same continent, yet separated by mountains and desert plains.

It was not until after the acquisition of Louisiana by the United States in 1803 that such a journey was accomplished, or even attempted. The chief city of the Mississippi Valley, in the newly acquired territory, was St. Louis; the principal settlement on the easterly side of the river, within the old boundaries of the United States, was Kaskaskia. Each of these places claims the credit of sending the first adventurers across the plains to meet the tide of Spanish colonization coming from the south, at Santa Fé.

In 1804, Mr. Morrison, an enterprising merchant of Kaskaskia, sent a man called Baptiste La Lande, a French creole, to the head-waters of the Platte, furnished with goods to trade with the Indians, and with directions, if it should be possible, to press on to Santa Fé. La Lande succeeded in sending in some Indians to the Spanish borders, who gave a report of the arrival of this stranger from the almost unknown east. A party of Mexicans on horseback conveyed him into the northern settlements near Taos, from where he traveled on to Santa Fé, selling his merchandise as he went. Pleased with the country, in which he obtained far higher prices than he had dreamed of elsewhere, and captivated by some of the bright-eyed brunettes of the city, he concluded to return no more, and settled down in the capital of the province.

Two years before La Lande left the banks of the Mississippi, James Pursley, or Purcell, an enterprising Kentuckian, who was by turns a hunter, trapper and trader, left St. Louis on a hunting expedition to the head-waters of the Osage river, with two companions. After three years of wanderings and many adventures, he finally reached the northern border of New Mexico, in company with a great party of Indians. Wishing to ascertain whether the Spaniards would receive them in a friendly way and enter into trade, the Indians sent Pursley, with a small escort, to Santa Fé as a kind of ambassador. The governor (Alencaster) acceded to the request, and shortly afterward the whole band followed its advance guard, and after some time spent in trading, set out on its return to the north.

But Pursley, tired of life among the savages, concluded to remain in Santa Fé. He arrived there in June, 1805, and settled down to the pursuit of his trade as a carpenter. Here Pike found him in 1807, and had a conversation which has given to Pursley the fame of being the first discoverer of the gold of Colorado. "He assured me," says Pike, "that he had found gold on the head of La Platte, and had carried some of the virgin mineral in his shot-pouch for months; but that being in doubt whether he should ever again behold the civilized world, he threw the sample away."

These two adventurous traders may be called the Fathers of the Santa Fé Trail, although their arrival in New Mexico was more the result of chance than of any calculation. The visit of Lieutenant Pike to Santa Fé in 1807 created much interest throughout the west, and many of the adventurous sons of the border yearned to follow the path which led to the ancient city.

The first real expedition was undertaken in 1812 by a company of about a dozen enterprising men of St. Louis, who fitted out a party under command of Robert McKnight. They arrived after various hardships, in safety, at Santa Fé, but only to encounter unexpected troubles. They were arrested as spies, their merchandise seized and confiscated; and they were themselves sent to Chihuahua, where they languished in rigorous confinement until the success of the republican movement under Iturbide brought their release.

In 1815, Auguste P. Chouteau and Julius DeMunn, from St. Louis, went to the head-waters of the Arkansas to trade with the Indians and the next year penetrated southward to Taos and Santa Fé, where they were well received by Governor Maynez. But shortly afterwards Allande became governor, and a change of policy took place; Chouteau and DeMunn were arrested on the Animas river, brought to Santa Fé, imprisoned for fifty days, and finally deprived of all their property.

Shortly after, in 1819, David Meriwether, an Indian trader, was captured on the Arkansas river and imprisoned for some time at Santa Fé. These events naturally prevented any further attempt at traffic across the plains until the overthrow of the Spanish authority by the Mexican revolution in 1821. By a strange chance of fortune the same David Meriwether who was imprisoned in Santa Fé in 1819, re-entered the city as American governor of New Mexico in 1853.

In 1821, an Ohio merchant named Glenn, arrived in Santa Fé with a small caravan, and in the same year, Captain William Becknell, who is now called the founder of the "Commerce of the Prairies," made an expedition from Franklin, Missouri, to the Rocky Mountains, to trade with the Indians, and concluded to turn south, and found at Santa Fé a far better market than among the Comanches. Returning that winter with the fruits of his enterprise, he raised a company of thirty friends, and with them and an assortment of goods which cost about $5,000, and was the largest venture of the kind yet made, started across the plains. They determined to try a more direct route, and so branched off from the Arkansas river at the point called "the Caches," intending to march directly southwest to Santa Fé. But this daring enterprise came near costing them their lives, for the unknown country was utterly devoid of water. Their scanty supply was soon exhausted, and the horrors of thirst took possession of them. They killed their dogs and cut off the ears of their mules in order to endeavor to find a moment's relief by drinking the warm blood of the animals.

Early in May, Colonel Cooper, a neighbor of Captain Becknell, left Missouri, about fifteen being in the party, and by pursuing the better-known route up the Arkansas, successfully made the journey. Down to 1824, all of the expeditions were on mule-back, and the amount of goods that could be transported was comparatively inconsiderable; but in the latter year a new departure was made by the employment of vehicles. The caravan which then started consisted of twenty-five wagons of different kinds, besides a number of pack-mules, and their success in making the trip gave a great impetus to the Santa Fé trade. The original cost of the goods brought by this caravan was $25,000 to $30,000.

From this time the trips across the plains became more frequent. The profits made on American goods were immense, because the only other route by which they could be received was by the sea to Vera Cruz, across the country to the city of Mexico, thence over the long and difficult road to El Paso, and finally by the semi-annual caravans up the Rio Grande, and crossing the Jornada, to Santa Fé. Plain domestic cottons sold as high as $2.00 or $3.00 per yard, on the plaza of the capital.

The occurrence of murderous attacks by Indians caused the government in 1827 to furnish an armed escort, but for some unexplained reason it was only repeated on special occasions thereafter, as in 1834 and in 1843.

Down to 1824 only pack-animals were employed; in 1824 and 1825 pack-animals and wagons; and commencing in 1826, nothing but wagons. Oxen were first used in 1830. The following statistics show the gradual increase in the business from its commencement in 1822 until 1843, when the trade was temporarily closed:

Years	Cost of Merchandise	No. Wagons	Men
1822	$ 15,000		70
1823	12,000		50
1824	35,000	26	100
1825	65,000	37	130
1826	90,000	60	100
1827	85,000	55	90
1828	150,000	100	200
1829	60,000	30	50
1830	120,000	70	140
1831	250,000	130	320
1832	140,000	70	150
1833	180,000	150	185

Years	Cost of Merchandise	No. Wagons	Men
1834	150,000	80	160
1835	140,000	75	140
1836	130,000	70	135
1837	150,000	80	160
1838	90,000	50	100
1839	250,000	130	250
1840	50,000	30	60
1841	150,000	60	100
1842	160,000	70	120
1843	450,000	230	350

In the beginning of the traffic across the plains, those engaged in it were nearly all Americans or French, from the western states; but gradually New Mexicans of wealth began to take part in the business, until in 1843 the greater part of the traders were New Mexicans.

While the time occupied in making the passage varied considerably according to circumstances, yet an average trip to Santa Fé, with loaded wagons, occupied about seventy days, and the return trip about forty days. The eastward loads were comparatively light, usually from 1,000 to 2,000 pounds, and the approaching winter compelled haste. On one occasion, F. X. Aubrey, a young man of Canadian descent, rode, on a wager, from Santa Fé to Independence in five days and ten hours; his own mare Nellie carrying him 150 miles of the distance.

Gregg, in his *Commerce of the Prairies,* gives a graphic account of the way in which the movements of the caravan were managed. The first business was to elect a "Captain of the Caravan," who directed the order of travel and designated the camping-ground. The proprietors furnished a full list of the wagons and men, and the caravan was then apportioned into about four divisions, each with a lieutenant in command, as they generally marched in four lines abreast.

The place of rendezvous for the caravan was usually Council Grove, the wagons leaving Independence at somewhat different times.

It was the custom when about 200 miles from Santa Fé to send a party of couriers ahead to that city to procure provisions and secure good store-houses. At the crossing of Red river, some part of the caravan frequently left the main body to proceed westerly to Taos; and a little further on they were met by the custom-house guard, who came to escort the caravan into Santa Fé to prevent smuggling.

San Francisco Street, Santa Fe, 1880.

When the caravan finally came in sight of Santa Fé, great excitement prevailed and the arrival produced a great deal of bustle in the city.

The wagons were soon discharged in the warerooms of the custom-house; and the weary travelers had time to take that recreation which a fatiguing journey of ten weeks had rendered so necessary.

The tariff duties of Mexico were extremely oppressive, averaging about 100 per cent upon the cost of an ordinary Santa Fé assortment. Those on cotton textures were particularly so. For a few years, Governor Armijo established a tariff of his own, entirely arbitrary—exacting $500 for each wagon-load, whether large or small, of fine or coarse goods! As might have been anticipated, the traders soon used only the largest wagons, drawn by ten or twelve mules, and omitted the coarser articles of trade. It was calculated that the amount collected each year at this time amounted to between $50,000 and $60,000.

The return trip usually commenced four or five weeks after the arrival at Santa Fé; generally about the 1st of September. Usually the caravan consisted of only thirty or forty wagons, a large portion of those taken out being disposed of in the country. The return cargo was silver bullion from Chihuahua—and in later years, gold-dust from the placers south of Santa Fé—buffalo-rugs, furs, coarse Mexican blankets and wool, the latter, however, hardly paying a fair freight, but being used to fill wagons which would otherwise have been empty.

Stories of tragedies on the plains, especially during the early days, could be multiplied almost indefinitely. Generally they resulted from the carelessness or over-confidence of the traders.

In 1846 the number of wagons in the caravan was 414, and the value of the merchandise transported was estimated at $1,752,250. After the American occupation the business of the Santa Fé Trail still further increased; new and large commercial establishments being founded at the capital city, from which a great part of northern Mexico as well as New Mexico and Arizona were supplied.

CHAPTER XVIII

Spanish and Mexican Governors

SPANISH GOVERNORS AND CAPTAINS GENERAL OF NEW MEXICO

Juan de Oñate, 1598-1608.
Pedro de Peralta, 1608.
Felipe Zotylo, 1621-8.
Manuel de Silva, 1629.
Fernando de Arguello, 1640.
Louis de Rosas, 1641.
—— Valdez, 1642.
Alonso Pacheco de Heredia, 1643.
Fernando de Arguello, 1645.
Luis de Guzman, 1647.
Hernando de Ugarte y la Concha, 1650.
Juan de Samaniego, 1653-4.
Enrique de Avila y Pacheco, 1656.
Bernardo Lopez de Mendizabal, 1660.
Diego de Peñalosa Briceno, 1661-4.
Fernando de Villanueva.
Juan de Medrano.
Juan de Miranda.
Juan Francisco de Treviño, 1675.
Antonio Otermin, 1679-83.
Domingo Jironza Petriz Cruzate, 1683-6.
Pedro Reneros de Posada, 1686-9.
Domingo Jironza Petriz Cruzate, 1689-91.
Diego de Vargas Zapata Lujan Ponce de Leon, 1691-7.
Pedro Rodriguez Cubero, 1697-1703.
Diego de Vargas Zapata Lujan Ponce de Leon, 1703-4.
Juan Paez Hurtado, acting, 1704-5.
Francisco Cuervo y Valdez, *ad interim*, 1705-7.
José Chacon Medina Salazar y Villaseñor, Marquez de la Peñuela, 1707-12.

Juan Ignacio Flores Mogollon, 1712-15.
Felix Martinez, *ad interim*, 1715-17.
Juan Paez Hurtado, acting, 1717.
Antonio Valverde y Cosio, *ad interim*, 1717-22.
Juan de Estrada y Austria (?), *ad interim*, 1721.
Juan Domingo de Bustamante, 1722-31.
Gervasio Cruzat y Góngora, 1731-6.
Enrique de Olavide y Micheleña, *ad interim*, 1736-9.
Gaspar Domingo de Mendoza, 1739-43.
Joaquin Codallos y Rabal, 1743-9.
Tomas Velez Cachupin, 1749-54.
Francisco Antonio Marin del Valle, 1754-60.
Mateo Antonio de Mendoza, acting, 1760.
Manuel Portillo Urrisola, acting, 1761-2.
Tomas Velez Cachupin, 1762-7.
Pedro Fermin de Mendinueta, 1767-78.
[Hereafter the title of Captain General is omitted.]
Francisco Trebol Navarro, acting, 1778.
Juan Bautista de Anza, 1778-89.
Fernando de la Concha, 1789-94.
Fernando Chacon, 1794-1805.
Joaquin del Real Alencaster, 1805-8.
Alberto Mainez, acting, 1807-8.
José Manrique, 1808-14.
Alberto Mainez, 1814-16.
Pedro Maria de Allande, 1816-18.
Facundo Melgares, 1818-22.

MEXICAN GOVERNORS
(With the title of Jefe Politico until 1837)

Antonio Viscarra, 1822.
Francisco Javier Chaves, 1823.
Bartolomé Baca, 1823 to September, 1825.
Antonio Narbona, 1825 to May, 1827.
Manuel Armijo, 1827-8.
Antonio Viscarra, acting, 1828.
José Antonio Chaves, 1828-31.
Santiago Abreu, 1831-3.
Francisco Sarracino, 1833-5.

SPANISH AND MEXICAN GOVERNORS. 115

Juan Rafael Ortiz, acting, 1834.
Mariano Chaves, acting, 1835, May to July.
Albino Perez, 1835-7. (Title of Governor from 18.37.)
Pedro Muñoz, acting, 1837-8.
José Gonzales, revolutionary governor, 1837-8.
Manuel Armijo, 1838-40, and till 1846.
Antonio Sandoval, acting, 1841.
Mariano Martinez de Lejanza, 1844-5.
José Chaves, acting, 1845.
Juan Bautista Vigil y Alarid, acting, 1846.

CHAPTER XIX

The American Occupation

The commencement of a war between Mexico and the United States naturally caused great excitement in New Mexico, particularly as the news of the commencement of hostilities in May 1846, was almost immediately followed by information that an expedition was being fitted out in Missouri for an attack on Santa Fé.

This was the American "Army of the West," which was ordered to rendezvous at Fort Leavenworth, under General Stephen W. Kearny, for the conquest of New Mexico and California. This army was composed of the First Dragoons, U. S. A., of which Kearny was colonel; a Missouri regiment under Colonel Doniphan; a battery of light artillery, commanded by Major Clark; two companies of infantry, and the La Clede rangers of St. Louis; the whole together comprising 1,658 men and sixteen pieces of ordnance.

The different parts of the little army did not really come together until they had crossed the plains and arrived at Bent's Fort, near the present village of Las Animas in Colorado. From here a small detachment was sent to the Taos valley to ascertain the disposition of the people, the main body going on by way of the Raton Pass.

The first habitations seen were on the banks of the Mora, at the ranch of James Bonney, who had recently settled there. On August 15 the army entered Las Vegas, then a comparatively new town, and here stopped long enough for the general to make a proclamation of pacific intentions towards the people, and to administer the oath of allegiance to the United States to the alcalde, Juan de Dios Maes, who was then confirmed in his office. Tecolote was the next town reached, and here similar proceedings were had, as well as at San Miguel, then the principal town east of the mountains,

Meanwhile General Armijo, the Mexican governor, after issuing a stirring proclamation calling on the people to rise and defend their homes, had marched from Santa Fé to the narrow pass to Cañoncito to prevent the passage of the American army. So strong was the position, that Kearny did not think of attacking it directly, but arranged to take a circuitous route which would carry him around it without great danger, and encamped near the ruins of Pecos with that intent on August 17. But, during the night, the Mexican army, largely made up of inexperienced volunteers, poorly armed, had heard such exaggerated accounts of the force of the Americans, that it became demoralized; many left for their homes, and Armijo, after a council of war with his chief officers, concluded to retire toward the south.

So the Americans found the main road open, and proceeded toward the capital unembarrassed except by the breastwork of trees that had been thrown across the cañon. Wishing to reach there in one day, especially as their provisions were almost exhausted, they made a forced march, and arrived at Santa Fé before night-fall, raising the stars and stripes over the palace, and then retiring to the high ground in the southeast part of the town, for a camp. This was on August 18. General Kearny and several officers came a little in advance and were received at the palace by the secretary and acting governor, Juan Bautista Vigil, who formally delivered to them the government of the city.

Few marches in history exceed in daring that of the little "Army of the West" across the plains. Consisting of less than two regiments of men, it marched nine hundred miles from its base of supplies, not seeing a habitation except Bent's Fort between Leavenworth and the Mora river; suffering greatly from lack of water, and with neither provisions nor money sufficient to procure them for so long a march.

The first business of General Kearny, after taking possession of Santa Fé, was to commence the building of Fort Marcy, on the heights overlooking the city; and then to establish a provisional government. On the morning of the 19th, he assembled the people in the Plaza, and addressed them in reassuring language, saying that the army came with peaceable intentions and kind feelings, that they would be secure in their persons, property and religion; announcing that he had taken possession of all New Mexico for the United States, and that "you are no longer Mexican subjects, you have become American citizens." This address was received with general satisfaction and was replied to by Juan Bautista Vigil, who accepted the new sovereignty in the name of the people.

Fearing that there might be a concentration of Mexican troops to the south, General Kearny marched with 725 mounted men down the Rio Grande valley as far as Tomé; being everywhere well received by the people and finding no enemies of any kind. On the 22d of September, he established a regular civil government by the appointment of Charles Bent, of Taos, as governor, Donaciano Vigil as secretary, and Francis P. Blair as district attorney, together with judges and other officials. Governor Bent was an old resident and married to a New Mexican. General Kearny also had a code of laws prepared and put in force, which is known as the Kearny Code, and is the basis of all the subsequent laws of New Mexico. Having thus provided for the government of the territory, General Kearny set out with his little army on September 26 for California, leaving Colonel Doniphan in command.

This latter officer had orders to march immediately to Chihuahua, but just as he was starting news arrived of an attack by Navajos on Polvadera, which induced a change of programme, and an expedition against those Indians was determined on; so that the troops who had come across the plains in hostility to the Mexicans, found their first active duty in their defense.

This was a matter difficult to explain to the Indian mind, which considered that the Americans and themselves were both at war with the same enemies, but Colonel Doniphan finally succeeded in having a treaty made by which they agreed to cease from all depredations. This accomplished he set out on his celebrated march to Chihuahua, on December 14, leaving the remaining troops in command of Colonel Sterling Price.

Scarcely a day had passed after his departure before rumors arose of an impending revolt by the people of the territory. In judging of this we are to remember that these people were Mexicans and that their mother country was at war with the

United States, so that from their point of view, it was an act of patriotism to attempt to drive from their soil these invaders of their country.

The leaders in the contemplated revolt were Diego Archuleta, who had been a member of the Mexican congress, and Tomas Ortiz, who had been high in command under Armijo, both men of large influence, and they were supported by many of the leading Mexicans of the north of the territory. The first general meeting was held on the 12th of December, when it was decided that the rising should take place one week from that day, when all Americans, and all Mexicans who had consented to hold office under the American governor, should be killed or driven out of the territory.

Everything was carefully arranged, and the attempt might have been successful, but that the time of action was postponed until Christmas eve. This delay was fatal to the project, for meanwhile information of the conspiracy was conveyed to the governor, who promptly arrested those suspected and rendered the attempt abortive.

However, the spirit of revolt was far from destroyed, and suddenly developed itself in a most unexpected manner. Supposing all danger to be passed, Governor Bent left Santa Fé on January 14, on a visit to his home in Taos. On the night of the 19th, a large body of men, partly Mexicans and party Pueblo Indians, attacked his residence and succeeded in killing not only the governor, but Sheriff Lee, Prefect Vigil, District Attorney Leal, Narciso Beaubien, a son of Judge Beaubien, and Pablo Jaramillo, a brother-in-law of the governor. At the same time attacks were made on the Americans at the Arroyo Hondo and Rio Colorado above Taos, and at Mora, a number being killed at each place.

The startling news of the assassination reached Colonel Price the next day, quickly followed by tidings of the approach of a large Mexican and Indian force to attack the capital. Very few troops were in Santa Fé; in fact, the number remaining in the whole territory was very small, and they were scattered at Albuquerque, Las Vegas, and other distant points. Delay meant destruction. Orders were sent to Albuquerque for the two companies stationed there to come northward, and Price himself determined to march immediately to meet the insurgent army.

All the force that he could muster was three hundred and ten men, including Captain Angney's company and a few other regular troops, and a volunteer company composed of nearly all the Americans in the city, under command of Colonel Ceran St. Vrain, who happened to be in Santa Fé at the time. In this latter company were also Manuel Chaves, Nicolas Pino, and some other prominent New Mexicans, who volunteered their services. They set out on January 23, nerved by the belief that there was no alternative but victory or annihilation. Scarcely had the little army passed Pojuaque, when they met the advance guard of the Mexicans, and soon after found the main body drawn up on the high bank of the Santa Cruz river just east of the town of that name. They were commanded by General Montoya, aided by Generals Tafoya and Chavez. Here a fierce battle took place. The Mexican army was large, but undisciplined and poorly provided with arms. They had, however, a great advantage in their position and in the occupancy of a number of adobe houses, which were practically fortresses. Nevertheless, by a vigorous charge in front and a flank attack by St. Vrain's volunteers, they were finally dislodged and forced to retreat, leaving thirty-six dead on the field, General Tafoya being among the number.

At Los Luceros the Americans were re-enforced by the arrival of Captain Burgwin's company of cavalry, which had hastened up from Albuquerque. At Embudo the Mexicans made another stand, in a narrow cañon, but were forced to abandon it, and retreated towards the north, finally concentrating at the pueblo of Taos, in the church of which, with walls from three to six feet thick, they fortified themselves.

Against this building the Americans, as soon as they arrived, directed their attack; but cannon-balls made little impression on the massive walls, so after two hours' bombardment they withdrew to the Mexican town of Fernandez de Taos, three miles distant. Early the next morning the attack was renewed, but was bravely met, and it was not until after a seven hours' struggle, in which the cannon were finally brought up within sixty yards of the church, that the stronghold was taken; and then with a loss of a number of soldiers and of the gallant Captain Burgwin, who was mortally wounded at the very wall. One hundred and fifty of the insurgents were killed, and the next day the entire pueblo surrendered.

This practically ended the revolt. General Montoya and fourteen others were tried for the murder of Governor Bent and the others killed on January 19, and were convicted and executed. Others were sentenced to be hung for treason; but the President promptly pardoned them on the ground that no Mexican could be guilty of treason against the United States while war actually existed between the two countries. A few outbreaks occurred at isolated points soon afterward, but later in the year the arrival in Santa Fé of large re-enforcements made any future revolt futile. At the same time the people began to see that they had really more freedom and better protection from the Indians, under the American flag, than that of Mexico, and gradually became reconciled to the change in government.

The treaty of Guadalupe Hidalgo ceded all New Mexico to the United States, at the same time constituting all of its people except those who preferred formally to retain their Mexican citizenship, citizens of the United States, with the full rights and privileges belonging to that character; and thus the territory and its people became an integral part of the Great American Republic.

On the death of Governor Bent, Donaciano Vigil succeeded him, as acting governor, and continued to be chief-executive until Colonel Washington was appointed military governor in 1848. Vigil was a man of large experience and excellent judgment, and conducted the affairs of the territory very satisfactorily.

CHAPTER XX

U. S. Provisional Government, 1846-51

Under the provisions of the Kearny Code, the first legislature of New Mexico commenced its session on December 6, 1847. The Council consisted of seven members, with Antonio Sandoval, of Bernalillo county, as president; and the House of twenty-one members, with W. Z. Angney as speaker.

This legislature could do little but local business, as the treaty of peace with Mexico was not yet signed, but it has been rendered famous by the excellent character of the message delivered by Governor Donaciano Vigil, especially relative to public education.

It passed an act providing for a convention to consider a permanent form of government for New Mexico, and the delegates for this purpose met on October 10, 1848. This convention continued in session four days, with Father Antonio José Martinez as president, and J. M. Giddings, secretary. It adopted a memorial to Congress asking for a regular territorial government, and declared against the introduction of domestic slavery.

In the next year the military governor called an election for delegates to a convention to frame a territorial form of government. This convention met on September 24, 1849, and organized by electing Antonio José (Padre) Martinez as president, and James H. Quinn, secretary. By a vote of 15 to 4 Hugh N. Smith was elected as delegate to congress, but failed to have the election recognized in Washington.

Meanwhile, Texas, which claimed all the territory east of the Rio Grande, sent Spruce M. Baird, as judge, to organize that district into a county to be called Santa Fé. But he was received with such opposition that he did not attempt to carry his instructions into effect. In tthe spring of 1850, they sent a second commissioner, Robert S. Neighbors, to organize counties of the state of Texas and to hold elections in them of local officers.

This created some excitement, but produced no practical result. Almost at the same time, however, it became well known that the President and his cabinet at Washington desired the people of California and New Mexico to organize state governments without delay, in order to settle the question of slavery within their borders, and thus allay the great national excitement on the subject.

A convention was consequently called by Colonel Munroe, the military governor, which met on May 15, and adopted a state constitution, which all concede to be an admirable instrument. The two features which naturally attract most attention are the clear declaration against slavery in the new state, and the appreciation shown of the value of public education. Besides the section of the constitution forever prohibiting slavery in New Mexico, there was a strong paragraph on that subject in the accompanying address, showing that slavery had always been the curse of the communities in which it existed. It should never be forgotten that this first constitutional convention in New Mexico, in which native New Mexicans composed over ninety per cent of the membership, took this high ground and maintained it courageously, although by so doing they were placing in jeopardy their own right to self-government.

This constitution was submitted to the people on the 20th of June, and adopted with substantial unanimity. At the same time state officers and a legislature were elected, Henry Connelly being chosen governor, and Manuel Alvarez, lieutenant-governor. The legislature met on July 1, 1850, and elected as United States senators Francis A. Cunningham and Richard H. Weightman, but, while Mr. Weightman was on his way to Washington to claim his seat in the senate the famous compromise measures of 1850 were passed by Congress, one feature of which was the act organizing New Mexico as a territory, with boundaries including the areas now embraced in New Mexico, Arizona, and southern Colorado. This Organic Act was passed September 9, 1850. Meanwhile a controversy arose between Alvarez, acting as state governor while Connelly was absent in the east, and Colonel Munroe, the military and civil governor of the territory. Both were able men and sustained their respective positions with vigor. However, any real conflict was avoided, until the news arrived by the slow mails across the plains that Congress had passed the Compromise measures, which settled the whole matter.

Under the Organic Act, the territory had regular civil officers appointed by the president. The first of these were James S. Calhoun, governor, and Hugh N. Smith, secretary. The judiciary was composed of Grafton Baker, John S. Watts and Horace Mower. Under these officers, a regular civil government was inaugurated on the third of March, 1851, and a legislative assembly was elected, which met in June, Padre Martinez, of Taos, being elected president of the Council, and Theodore Wheaton, a prominent lawyer, speaker of the House.

From that time, the form of government continued for sixty years without any material change; the principal additional officer being the surveyor-general, appointed under an act of 1855, which delegated to him large powers in determining questions relating to Spanish and Mexican land grants.

CHAPTER XXI

The Territorial Period, 1851-1912

This period of sixty years will be considered briefly under the administrations of the successive governors; but for convenience of treatment matters connected with churches, schools, and newspapers are arranged in groups in a distinct chapter, in order to present a connected view of each subject.

Indian Fighters

During much of this period, as well as through the preceding Mexican era, there were constantly recurring Indian hostilities, incursions into the border settlements and even to the Rio Grande valley by bands of Navajos, Utes and Apaches, and expeditions to recover captives and animals or to inflict punishment, undertaken by the people of the territory. From among the most noted "Indian Fighters" who were prominent in these wars, we have selected four for illustration—José Maria Chavez, Manuel Chaves, Roman A. Baca and Kit Carson.

José Maria Chavez was born earlier than either of the other great Indian fighters, yet his life extended over so many years that he was the survivor of all of them. He was born at Santa Clara, September 25, 1801, and he died at Abiquiu, November 22, 1902, aged 101 years and 58 days. His ancestors were officers with De Vargas, and his own career began early, as he held three military offices under the King of Spain before Mexican independence in 1822. During the Mexican era he was constantly in office and became a Brigadier-General. He took part in eleven campaigns against the Indians, in five of which he was commander-in-chief. All the northwestern frontier is full of stories of his daring and courage. The portrait here reproduced was taken when he was 95 years old.

Manuel Chaves was born at Atrisco, October 18, 1818, and belonged to one of the most distinguished families in New Mexico. When only 16 years old he took part in a campaign against the Navajos, and from then until his death, in 1889, he was the favorite commander in expeditions against the Indians, whether Navajos, Utes or Apaches. After the killing of Gov.

General Jose Maria Chavez at Age of 95, 1801-1902.

Bent, in 1847, he enlisted in St. Vrain's company of volunteers, and served during the Taos expedition. In 1862 it was he who guided the American troops to the rear of Sibley's army at

Apache Cañon, and thus secured the victory of Glorieta. Many romantic incidents of his life are narrated by Lummis in "A New Mexico David." His bravery was beyond description and brought him the name of El Leoncito (the little lion).

Colonel Manuel Chaves, 1818-1889.

Roman A. Baca was born at Cebolleta, in 1833, and was the half brother of Manuel Chaves, they having the same mother. The early campaigns of Don Roman were on expeditions commanded by his elder brother, and he was thus brought up in a school of courage and daring adventure. Among other warlike accomplishments, he was a wonderful shot with a bow and arrow. Born and brought up on the Navajo frontier, he learned

Hon. Roman A. Baca, 1833-1899.

all the art of the Indian and exceeded him in skill. Many a contest in markmanship was held with the most noted Indian champions, but young Baca always carried off the prize. In

years of age he joined a caravan bound for Santa Fé in charge of Ceran St. Vrain. He was a trapper, a miner, a hunter, a courier, a guide, an explorer and a fighter. He was on three expeditions with Fremont, he traversed the whole Rocky Mountain region, was with Sutter at Sacramento and Kearny at San Diego. His adventures with Indians would fill a volume. He was Colonel of the First New Mexico Cavalry, and became a Brigadier General. He died May 28, 1868, at Fort Lyon.

JAMES S. CALHOUN (1851)

was the first governor of New Mexico appointed by the President under the regular territorial government. He was inaugurated on March 3, 1851, and at the same time William S. Allen became secretary, Hugh N. Smith not having been confirmed.

Governor Calhoun was already a resident of Santa Fé, as he had been Indian Agent for New Mexico since July, 1849, and had shown himself a most intelligent and diligent official. Soon after his inauguration he called an election for the first regular territorial legislature, which convened in the Governor's Palace on June 2, and held a second session on December 1 of the same year.

Governor Calhoun's position was anything but a bed of roses. The situation was new, and the limits of the authority of the civil and military officials not yet closely determined. Troubles with the Indians were of constant occurrence. The governor was also Indian Agent and endeavored to keep the peace and prevent depredations. Col. E. V. Sumner, in military command of the department, had different views of the method of procedure. The governor graphically explains his position in an official report, in which he is "without a dollar in our territorial treasury, without munitions of war, without authority to call out our milita, without the co-operation of the military authorities." Finally he started on a journey to Washington in May, 1852, and died on the route. Meanwhile Colonel Sumner built Ft. Defiance, Ft. Union, and other army posts.

WILLIAM CARR LANE (1852)

Governor Lane had been an army surgeon and afterwards mayor of St. Louis. He arrived in 1852, endeavored to pacify

later life he was chosen leader in many expeditions against the Indians. He held various civil offices, was Speaker of the House of Representatives, Penitentiary Commissioner, etc., but

Kit Carson, 1809-1868.

his great celebrity was won as an Indian fighter. He died in Santa Fé in 1899.

Kit Carson's life is like a long romance, but cannot be given here. He was born in Kentucky in 1809, and when seventeen

the Indians by supplying them with rations, issued a proclamation claiming the Mesilla valley as part of New Mexico, and became a candidate for Congress before election but failed of success, a small majority being given to José Manuel Gallegos (Padre Gallegos of Albuquerque). Soon after this disappointment he left for the east, leaving W. S. Messervy, who had been appointed secretary, in charge of the territory, and never returned.

DAVID MERIWETHER (1853)

The next governor was David Meriwether, appointed by President Pierce at the beginning of his administration in 1853. He was a Kentuckian by residence but had had a very romantic experience in the far west, and in 1819 had been captured by the Spaniards and confined as a prisoner for some time in the Palace. He made an intelligent, practical governor, but during his administration of four years there was incessant war with the surrounding Indian tribes.

During this administration the Gadsden Purchase was made from Mexico, by which a strip of territory from the Rio Grande to the Colorado river was added to the domain of the United States.

A notable event of this period was the killing of F. X. Aubrey by Maj. R. H. Weightman, in the store of the Mercures on the south side of the Plaza in Santa Fé. This occurred on August 18, 1854, just after Aubrey had returned from California, in twenty-nine days from San José to Peralta, demonstrating the feasibility of a railroad route to the Pacific. He had previously achieved celebrity by his record-breaking ride on the Santa Fé Trail before referred to.

In 1854 Congress made an appropriation of $50,000 for the construction of the capitol, this being in addition to $20,000 appropriated in 1850, with which the foundation was laid. The structure was now carried up one and a half stories and thus remained, roofless, until it was utilized for the Tertio-Millennial exposition in 1883, and subsequently completed for United States offices.

W. W. H. Davis, who had previously been United States attorney, was Secretary during much of Governor Meriwether's term, and wrote several books on New Mexican history. He was acting-governor for nearly a year before the arrival of the next governor.

ABRAHAM RENCHER (1857)

was appointed by President Buchanan at the beginning of his presidential term, and served for four years. He was a lawyer who had been a member of Congress and also in the diplomatic service.

During this administration the Indian difficulties continued, especially with the Navajos. In 1859 and 1860 nearly 300 citizens were killed by the Indians, and on February 7, 1860, they made a bold attempt to capture Ft. Defiance itself. This was followed by an active campaign by Colonel Canby, which ended in victory and a temporary cessation of hostilities.

The United States Land Office was established at this time and the Santa Fé office was opened on November 25, 1858. The surveyor general's office had been established in 1854, and William Pelham continued as its head until 1860.

On the last Monday in December, 1859, the Historical Society of New Mexico was organized, with Col. John R. Grayson as president, Chief Justice Kirby Benedict delivering the opening address.

HENRY CONNELLY (1861)

Governor Connelly was a man of large experience in the southwest, and the first citizen of New Mexico to be appointed governor under the Organic Act, and the only one during forty-four years. He was originally a physician in Kentucky, but went to Chihuahua in 1828, and at the close of the Mexican war settled in Santa Fé, and lived there and at Peralta during the remainder of his life. He was thus well equipped by experience for the duties of the governorship. He was appointed by President Lincoln early in 1861, and was reappointed in 1865, continuing in office until his death in July, 1866.

On February 24, 1863, Congress passed the act establishing the territory of Arizona out of the western portion of New Mexico, and on December 31 of that year the newly appointed officials of Arizona organized its territorial government at Navajó

Springs, just within its boundaries, and afterwards established the capital at Prescott. Col. J. Francisco Chaves was the escort of the officers of the new territory.

The most important events of Governor Connelly's administration were those connected with the War of the Rebellion. Throughout the whole trouble he was an ardent Union man and his large acquaintance gave him much influence in preventing defections from the Union cause.

Mr. Floyd, of Virginia, when secretary of war, had arranged for the betrayal of the Union troops in New Mexico, by putting in command Colonel W. W. Loring and George B. Crittenden, both of whom, when the Rebellion opened, abandoned their trusts and went to Texas after vainly endeavoring to seduce the men under their command.

The first military operations were in July, 1861, when Lieutenant-Colonel John R. Baylor, marching into New Mexico from El Paso, took possession of Mesilla.

On August 1 Colonel Baylor issued a proclamation organizing a new territory which he named Arizona, to consist of all the part of New Mexico south of the 34th parallel of latitude, as a portion of the Confederate States, and announcing himself as governor.

During the winter of 1861-2, the Confederate leaders arranged a programme of campaign for the far west, which was intended to separate the Pacific states from the rest of the country, and finally take possession of them with their long line of sea-coast and wealth of gold. The plan was to send an army northerly from Texas to capture the great stores of arms and munitions at Fort Union, and then to proceed into Colorado, thus cutting all the lines of communication between the east and the far west. The importance of this campaign can hardly be over-estimated. During the fall the Texan forces were gathered at El Paso, and by New Year included 2,300 men, commanded by Gen. H. H. Sibley, who was another officer that had been stationed in New Mexico and abandoned the service of his country.

On December 20 General Sibley issued a proclamation, skilfully worded to seduce the New Mexican people from their allegiance to the Union, and also offering inducements to military officers and soldiers to desert their flag.

The native people of New Mexico, with very few exceptions, were thoroughly loyal to the Union throughout the entire war. The territorial legislature authorized Governor Connelly to call out the whole force of the territory for the protection of its soil and people.

On the defection of Colonel Loring in 1861, General Canby, a brave and patriotic officer, was placed in command of the department, with Lieutenant-Colonel Roberts next in rank; and under them in the spring of 1862 were 900 men all told. Two regiments of New Mexico volunteers were raised, of one of which Ceran St. Vrain was Colonel, Kit Carson, lieutenant-colonel, and J. Francisco Chaves, major; the other being commanded by Col. Miguel Pino.

The Union force was concentrated at Fort Craig, when in February the Southern army under General Sibley, about 2,500 strong, appeared in the valley of the Rio Grande. In the battle of Valverde, on the east side of the Rio Grande, on February 21, Canby's army failed in its object and he was forced to re-cross the river to Fort Craig. Sibley then marched up the valley and occupied Albuquerque; and, there being no means of resistance at hand, the United States officials evacuated Santa Fé on March 3, and retired to Fort Union, Sibley's army occupying the capital a week later.

Meanwhile, Governor Gilpin had sent the First Regiment of Colorado Volunteers, under Colonel John P. Slough, southward from Denver to the aid of the threatened territory; and after a hard march, they arrived at Fort Union on March 11, and marched with very little delay along the old trail towards Santa Fé. They were joined by a few companies of regular troops and by a considerable number of volunteers, and on the 20th of March met the advancing Confederate army at Apache Cañon or Glorieta. The battle fought here, though hardly known to history, was the decisive conflict which settled the result of the war in the Rocky Mountain country. On the first day only a part of each army was engaged, and the contest was indecisive.

Early next morning, Captain Manuel Chaves led four hundred men under Major Chivington by a circuitous path to the rear of the Confederate position. In the main battle, which was fiercely contested and lasted five hours, Sibley succeeded in driv-

THE TERRITORIAL PERIOD. 135

ing the Union soldiers back some distance to Koslowsky's Ranch, but at this moment Chivington fell upon the rear of the Confederate force and destroyed its wagons and supplies. The news of this loss demoralized the Texan army, the fate of the day was changed, and Sibley commenced a retreat southerly, evacuating Santa Fé on April 8, and proceeding down the valley. He was closely followed, and was greatly embarrassed by want of supplies; on April 15, at Peralta, he was attacked by the Union forces and forced to retreat rapidly to El Paso to avoid capture. At this battle of Peralta the New Mexican company commanded by Maj. José D. Sena gained special credit.

This ended the campaign, and indeed was the end of the war in New Mexico. In July, the first detachments of the "California Column," which had marched across the deserts of Arizona, reached Ft. Thorne, and soon after the main body under Gen. James H. Carleton arrived at Mesilla. It included about 2,350 men, and its remarkable march across the desert from the Pacific to the Rio Grande is one of the most gallant achievements of the entire war. Its presence prevented further inroads, if they had been intended.

The alacrity with which the people of New Mexico flocked to the standard of the Union during the years from 1861 to 1865, will always be a source of pride to the Sunshine State. The soldiers' monument, erected by order of three legislatures, in the center of the Plaza at Santa Fé, fitly commemorated the loyalty and bravery of those who fell in defense of the Union in this campaign of 1862.

The people showed themselves as loyal as any in the Nation. During the Rebellion, out of her total population of 93,567, New Mexico sent 6,561 men into the army. The total number of volunteers from the territories now comprising the six states of North Dakota, South Dakota, Washington, Montana, Idaho, and Wyoming, was 1,170. Colorado sent but 4,903, and Nebraska, Oregon, and Nevada, taken together, contributed but 6,047, being 500 less than New Mexico alone. In fact, the official statistics show that no state of the Union contributed such a percentage of its population to the Union army as did New Mexico. Surely this is a record of which her children can be proud.

Robert B. Mitchell (1866)

Governor Mitchell was appointed by President Johnson shortly after the death of Governor Connelly. He was a man of varied experience, a lawyer in Ohio, a lieutenant in the Mexican War, an active free-state man in Kansas, a colonel and finally a brigadier general in the Union army. He became governor of New Mexico in 1866, and served until 1869. His administration was a troublous one through its entire period. He was out of harmony with the legislature, and exercised the veto power, which was then absolute, unsparingly. The legislature appealed to Congress and the Organic Act was amended by providing that a veto could be overridden by a two-thirds vote. He invoked criticism by long absences from the territory, and the legislature went so far finally as to ask for his removal.

On December 15, 1867, occurred the tragic death of Chief Justice Slough (the Colonel Slough of the Colorado Volunteers) at the hands of Col. W. L. Rynerson in the office of the Exchange hotel, then called the "Fonda," in Santa Fé.

It was during this administration that the Navajo Indians, who had been carried across New Mexico to the Bosque de Apache reservation, on the Pacos river, in 1864 and 1865, were allowed to return to their old home near the Arizona line, by the treaty signed by General Sherman on behalf of the Indian Peace Commission, on June 1, 1867.

William A. Pile (1869)

On the accession of General Grant to the presidency, he appointed, as governor, William A. Pile, of Missouri, afterwards minister to Venezuela.

It is one of the curiosities of history that this gentleman, who is uniformly well spoken of by those best acquainted with his character, should be known in New Mexico principally from his supposed connection with the sale of a portion of the Spanish archives for use as wrapping paper. Probably that connection was very slight; but it is certain that quantities of old documents were sold or given away to merchants for that purpose, and that an indignation meeting was held in Santa Fé to protest against such vandalism.

During his administration the soldiers' monument in Santa Fé was completed, and Lincoln and Colfax counties were created, telegraphic communication with the east was opened on July 8, 1869, and the First National Bank of Santa Fé, the oldest in the entire southwest, was chartered and organized.

MARSH GIDDINGS (1871)

Under appointment by President Grant, Marsh Giddings succeeded Governor Pile in the executive office in 1871, and continued as governor until his death, on June 3, 1875.

In 1871, John Martin, a veteran of two wars, discovered water in the center of the Jornada del Muerto, at Martin's Well or Aleman, which was of such importance to the public that the legislature specially recognized the benefit thereby conferred.

In August, 1872, the Second National Bank of Santa Fé was established.

In 1873, the United States military road from Santa Fé to Taos was completed, up the Rio Grande through Santa Cruz, Los Luçeros, La Joya, and Rinconada, and took the place of the old route further east. In 1861 Congress appropriated $15,000 for this road, and subsequently $25,000 for its completion.

Perhaps the most important events in this administration were the earnest efforts made to secure statehood, both in New Mexico and Washington.

In 1872, the legislature took up the subject early in the session and passed "An Act Providing for a General Election for the Purpose of Submitting to a Vote of the People a State Constitution and State Officers."

The constitution that was thus submitted was printed in a pamphlet of forty-seven pages and was a comprehensive document, creditable to those who prepared and adopted it. It was approved by a majority of the voters at the election, but soon after there appeared in the *New Mexican* an editorial article, evidently inspired by Governor Giddings, which gave a reason or rather an excuse, for letting the whole subject drop.

So this attempt at statehood, which occupied the attention of two legislatures, and caused a constitution to be prepared, printed, approved by the legislature, and submitted to the people, died without any good cause.

While these proceedings were taken in New Mexico, Congress had been no less active in considering the subject.

In 1869 an attempt was made, though not by New Mexicans, to transform the territory into a state called Lincoln; but this project was defeated in the senate.

In the 40th Congress, Delegate J. Francisco Chaves made a vigorous speech in favor of statehood and in defense of the people against unjust criticism.

In the 43d Congress (1873-5) an enabling act was introduced by Hon. S. B. Elkins, then delegate from New Mexico, and on the 21st of May, 1874, he delivered a carefully prepared speech on the subject. The bill passed the House by the remarkable vote of 160 to 54, and was sent to the Senate for concurrence. In that body it finally passed on February 24, 1875, by the decisive majority of 32 to 11, with a slight amendment. It was then that the incident occurred which has become historic as the "Elkins handshake," and again dashed the cup of success from the lips of the people. When the bill was returned to the House, after passing the Senate with amendments, but ten days of the session remained, and a two-thirds vote was necessary if the bill was to be considered at all.

Just at this time Mr. Burrows, of Michigan, made a powerful speech on political subjects, which at that period, on account of its allusions to the war, was called a "bloody shirt" speech. Mr. Elkins, who had been conversing in the lobby, had not heard a word of the speech, but happened to re-enter the chamber just as Mr. Burrows had concluded and was receiving the congratulations of a crowd of members. Filled with his spirit of cordiality, Mr. Elkins shook hands with the speaker with characteristic vigor. This was observed by a number of southern members whose feelings had been much excited by the speech, and they instantly concluded that they would lend no aid to the New Mexico bill, which it was understood would bring Mr. Elkins speedily to the Senate; and so the enabling act was lost.

On the death of Governor Giddings, Secretary William G. Ritch acted as governor until the inauguration of Governor Axtell. He was a very progressive man, and for years gave his best efforts to the establishment of an effective public school system.

THE TERRITORIAL PERIOD. 139

SAMUEL B. AXTELL (1875)

Governor Axtell was appointed by President Grant, and inaugurated as governor on July 30, 1875. He had been a member of Congress from California for two terms, and was governor of Utah at the time of his appointment to New Mexico. He was a man of the positive character which makes warm friends and bitter enemies.

During his official term the Lincoln county war between rival cattlemen and their adherents was a prominent feature. The contending factions were named after Murphy and McSwain, who were the leading cattle owners of that section. In this "war" a number of men were killed and the whole southeast of the territory was involved. A somewhat similar condition existed in Colfax county where the cowboy element was strong. Great excitement was occasioned in 1875 by the murder of Rev. F. J. Tolby, a Methodist minister, on the road from Cimarron to Elizabethtown; and an attempt was made to connect Governor Axtell with that outrage. Party feeling ran very high and numerous charges against the governor were forwarded to Washington, and special agents were sent from there to investigate. In the calmer judgment of history each side misjudged the other, but the result was a determination by the national administration to change the principal New Mexico officials. Accordingly, in the fall of 1878, Governor Axtell was superseded by Gen. Lew Wallace, and Col. Sidney M. Barnes, of Kentucky, was appointed United States attorney.

Subsequently, in 1882, Governor Axtell was appointed chief justice, and performed the duties of that office to the general satisfaction of the people.

In 1876 New Mexico suffered a considerable loss of territory by the change of the northern boundary whereby the new state of Colorado acquired everything north of the 37th parallel of latitude.

LEWIS WALLACE (1878)

Governor Wallace was appointed by President Hayes with instructions to restore tranquility in the territory and to reform any abuses he might find prevailing. He was inaugurated October 1, 1878. He was a man of ability and reputation, having served in the Mexican war as lieutenant, and as major-general and corps commander in the War of the Rebellion.

The first special business undertaken by Governor Wallace was the pacification of the Lincoln county troubles. With this object,

Governor Lew Wallace.

he visited Lincoln itself and had several interviews with Billy the Kid and other active participants. The war was not concluded, however, until the killing of the "Kid," whose real name was William H. Bonney, by Pat Garrett, sheriff of Lincoln county, on July 14, 1881.

During his administration, the Atchison, Topeka and Santa Fé railroad entered the territory, affording direct connection with the east. This line reached Las Vegas on July 1, 1879, and Santa Fé on February 9, 1880. On its completion to the capital a brilliant celebration was held, the last four spikes being driven by the governor, chief justice, commanding general, and chairman of the county commission, with address of congratulation by Chief Justice Prince. The Denver and Rio Grande railroad was built south from Antonito as far as Española. This advance of the railroads stimulated all kinds of enterprises; street railways, modern hotels, gas works, and large commercial houses were constructed; mining enterprises covered the territory; many churches and schools were established, and general incorporation acts for municipalities, religious and charitable societies, and foreign corporations were enacted. On February 15, 1880, the legislature passed an act establishing a Bureau of Immigration, which organized on April 15. Many churches and schools were established, as will appear elsewhere.

On December 27, 1880, the Historical Society of New Mexico was organized and incorporated, the original society having suspended operations during the war. For thirty years this society has had its home in the Palace at Santa Fé under national and territorial authorities, and has accumulated a collection of New Mexican antiquities and historic material absolutely invaluable, and which, but for its faithful efforts, would have been taken from New Mexico long ago.

The event which most closely identifies Governor Wallace with New Mexico was the completion of his famous work, *Ben Hur*, by the writing of the sixth, seventh and eighth books in his bed room back of the executive office in the Palace, which has since been known as the "Ben Hur Room" and has become a Mecca for tourists.

On the election of General Garfield as president, Governor Wallace applied for a foreign diplomatic position and was appointed minister to Turkey.

LIONEL A. SHELDON (1881)

Governor Sheldon was appointed by President Garfield soon after his inauguration and assumed office May 15, 1881. He was a personal friend of the president, having been lieutenant-colonel of the Ohio regiment of volunteers of which General Garfield was colonel. After the war he served three times in Congress from Louisiana.

Governor Sheldon succeeded finally in what appeared to be his special desire, which was the building of a penitentiary to accommodate the increasing number of condemned criminals. In the legislature of 1884 a bill was also passed for the erection of a capitol in Santa Fé, and a commission was appointed for that purpose.

The governor gave much attention to organizing the militia as a protection not only against the lawless element that had entered the territory in connection with railroad construction, but also against the Indians, who were disposed to be aggressive. His term of office covered a period of active business and speculation in New Mexico. On the 13th of July, 1882, the Santa Fé Board of Trade was organized and incorporated, being the first commercial organization in the Southwest.

In 1883 there was held in Santa Fé a great historic celebration called the "Tertio Millennial," which exceeded anything of the kind yet attempted in America. The regular programme covered thirty-three days, during which each important Indian pueblo and tribe was represented by forty of its people, who exhibited their ceremonials and dances in the genuine costumes required by their religion or custom. The celebration began with a three days' historic pageant of gorgeous magnificence. It really engrossed the greater part of the year, and while a financial failure, was well worth all that it cost.

EDMUND G. ROSS (1885)

The democratic party having regained power by the election of Grover Cleveland, Edmund G. Ross was appointed governor, and assumed office June 15, 1885. Remembering the Pueblo tradition that Montezuma would some time appear at break of day to bless his people, Governor Ross took the oath of office exactly at sunrise, in the Palace, Governor Sheldon having been roused from his slumbers for that purpose.

Governor Ross was a man of strong opinions and courage, and of the temperament that rather rejoices in opposition. In early life he left Wisconsin to take part in the free state movement in Kansas and was an active participant in the Border War of those days. In 1861 he naturally entered the Union Army, did active duty as captain and major, and made an enviable record. From 1867 to 1871 he was United States senator, filling the unexpired term of Senator James H. Lane. It was then that he met the crisis of his life, in the impeachment trial of President Johnson. Party feeling was at fever heat and the republicans of Kansas were practically unanimous in opposition to Johnson. Senator Ross believed that a political conviction would revolutionize the government, and in the face of a storm of opposition he had the courage to cast the decisive vote which ended the impeachment. His enemies attributed this to every bad motive, including corruption, and he left office with scarcely a friend. As governor he had the same disregard for public opinion, that he showed in the senate. Absolutely honest and well-meaning but proud of his firmness, he antagonized his own party as well as the republican legislature, and was soon nearly powerless to accomplish anything.

Three important laws were past in 1889, one establishing a University, an Agricultural College, a School of Mines, and an Insane Asylum; Chapter 30, establishing a financial system for the territory; and Chapter 99, providing for a constitutional convention.

On January 9, 1886, at a meeting of lawyers, presided over by Hon. H. L. Waldo, the Bar Association of New Mexico was organized, with 19 members. Since then it has continually increased in membership and influence, and has become a recognized power in legislation.

L. BRADFORD PRINCE (1889)

The election of President Harrison returned the republicans to power and L. Bradford Prince was appointed governor, and he was inaugurated on April 17, on the west side of the capitol.

Gov. Prince had been a member of the Assembly of New York for five terms, and also of the Senate of that State; had come to New Mexico as Chief Justice in 1879, and served in that capacity under Presidents Hayes, Garfield and Arthur. He had been the first president of the Bureau of Immigration, and thus was well informed as to all parts of the Territory. The most pressing subject at that time was Public Education. The University, Agricultural College, and School of Mines were immediately built and opened, by boards appointed by the governor and of which he was an active member; and during his administration the Normal institutions at Silver City and at Las Vegas, and the Military Institute at Roswell, were established. Even more important to the people at large was the inauguration of a modern public school system for the whole territory, with a superintendent of public instruction at its head, in 1891. Under this system the cause of general education has advanced with remarkable rapidity, down to the present. The native New Mexican people had larger recognition in important appointments than ever before.

A convention to formulate a state constitution was elected in August and commenced its session September 3, 1889. Unfortunately, owing to dissatisfaction with the apportionment of members, the chairman of the democratic committee advised his party friends to take no part in the election and consequently but one prominent democrat, Judge Trimble, participated in the convention, and very few advocated the excellent constitution which was submitted to the people. The result was its rejection by the decisive vote of 16,180 to 7,493, and a long delay in the attainment of statehood.

Another very pressing matter was the settlement of land grant titles. For years Congress had been importuned to take action, but in vain. As increased immigration and prosperity were impossible under this incubus of uncertainty, the governor finally appointed a committee of fifty to go to Washington and endeavor to obtain favorable action. Twenty-five actually went, paying their own expenses. They arrived on April 25, 1890, and remained a month, with the governor as chairman. They appeared before congressional committees, cabinet officers and the president, and induced the latter to send a special message to Congress on the subject on July 1. The result was the establishment of the Court of Private Land Claims by an act approved March 3, 1891. This court consisted of seven judges, continued in existence until June 30, 1904, and finally settled all grant titles in the southwest.

This period was one of unusual business prosperity. All the principal industries of the territory were fostered and flourished. The public finances were very satisfactory. In 1890 the territorial auditor reported a surplus of $40,000 in the treasury, and

First Capitol, After Fire, May, 1892.

the reduction of the bonded debt of the territory began at this time, $30,000 of penitentiary bonds being paid off and canceled. So high was the credit of New Mexico that the territory had to pay 117 for the bonds thus paid off.

On May 12, 1892, the beautiful capitol building in Santa Fé was destroyed by fire, probably of incendiary origin. Almost all the public documents of value were saved, including the Spanish and Mexican archives. The governor's office was transferred to its old home in the palace, and the other territorial officials found temporary accommodations until the completion of the new capitol in 1900.

WILLIAM T. THORNTON (1893)

Grover Cleveland being again president of the United States, a democrat was naturally to be appointed governor in the spring of 1893, and the choice fell on William T. Thornton, who had been a resident of New Mexico since 1877, and prominent in legislative and legal affairs.

Through his entire administration he devoted himself to the punishment of crime, especially of murders, which had become alarmingly frequent. Two of these cases were especially conspicuous, that of Francisco Chavez, sheriff of Santa Fé county, and of John Dougherty, former sheriff of Mora. There was also a flagrant murder at the bridge in Las Vegas and the mysterious disappearance of a man named Silva and his family in the same town. In every instance the guilty parties were finally discovered, and the vigor of the prosecutions did much to stop the wave of crime that seemed flowing over the territory. Nineteen criminals were executed during the four years' term, and a large number of convictions for crimes punishable by imprisonment were obtained.

The Columbian Exposition at Chicago was held in 1893, and New Mexico was very creditably represented there by a territorial building and a fine display of its varied products. It gained a valuable reputation by exhibiting the finest oats in the United States and the best wheat in the entire world, and receiving prizes accordingly.

As an outgrowth of work for this Exposition, a unique organization, known as the Woman's Board of Trade, was formed in Santa Fé in 1903. From that time it has done the principal civic work in that city. It has entire charge of the plaza, attends to the public charities, manages the cemetery and has erected a fine library building in which it conducts a free circulating library.

In 1895 the legislature passed an act for the rebuilding of the capitol by a commission appointed by the governor. The sum of $75,000 was appropriated for the purpose, together with the use of old capitol material and of convict labor.

The struggle for statehood during this administration and during the next ten years presents a succession of attempts, regularly begun at the opening of each new Congress, carried on with more or less vigor, with apparent excellent prospects of success, usually resulting in the passage of the bill by the House of Representatives and its reference in the Senate to the committee on territories. Sometimes there would be public hearings by a committee; usually the delegate would make at least one speech begging for tardy justice to his people, and then at some stage of the procedure a snag was encountered and the bill died at the end of the session because it could not overcome the obstacle in time.

MIGUEL A. OTERO (1897)

The election of President McKinley brought the Republicans again into power, and Miguel A. Otero was appointed governor in 1897. He was the son of the Miguel A. Otero who was delegate in Congress for three terms, from 1855 to 1861.

The most important event in this administration was the participation of New Mexicans in the Spanish-American War in 1898. Immediately after the proclamation of the president for 125,000 volunteers, there was a rush of New Mexicans to enter the military service.

The quota assigned to New Mexico consisted of four troops of a regiment commanded by Leonard Wood as colonel and Theodore Roosevelt as lieutenant colonel, and known as the Rough Riders; and they were mustered into the service with great promptitude in Santa Fé. The major and captains were as follows:

Major, Henry B. Hersey
Troop E—Captain, Frederick Muller
Troop F—Captain, Maximiliano Luna
Troop G—Captain, W. H. H. Llewellyn
Troop H—Captain, George Curry

The regiment was brought together at San Antonio, Texas, and from there, on May 29, 1898, forwarded to Tampa en route to Cuba. One company had to remain in Florida, and the troop of Captain Curry encountered that bad fortune. No one regretted this more than themselves. The others embarked on

June 14, and on the 22d landed on the island near Santiago. The rest of their career is national history, and no brighter page is to be found than that which chronicles the gallantry of the New Mexico troops at Las Guasimas, and San Juan Hill. According to Colonel Roosevelt's own statement, the first standards planted on the summit were those of the three troops from the Sunshine State.

Under the second call for volunteers, a battalion of four companies marched forth from New Mexico. They were mustered into service in July, 1898, and remained in camp in Kentucky and Georgia for a considerable time, but had no opportunity to meet the enemy. This, however, should not detract from their reputation, as they were not only ready but anxious for active service.

These companies were as follows:
Company E, Albuquerque—Captain, John Borradaile
Company F, Las Vegas—Captain, W. C. Reid
Company G, Santa Fé—Captain, William Strover
Company H, Las Cruces—Captain, A. B. Fall

During this period the territory continued to increase in population, especially by the settlement of the eastern portion and the Estancia valley, which had been considered sections only adapted to grazing, but which were now rapidly covered with homesteads. There were constant attempts to secure statehood, without result.

The most important legislation was the passage by Congress of the act of June 21, 1898, championed by Delegate H. B. Fergusson, donating to the territory large areas of public lands for educational and other purposes, in advance of statehood.

At the Trans-Mississippi Exposition at Omaha in 1898 and the great Louisiana Purchase Exposition at St. Louis in 1904, the territory was officially represented and made very creditable exhibitions of its resources and products.

In 1900 the new capitol was completed, in a very satisfactory and creditable manner; and on June 4 it was formally opened, with an address by Ex-Governor Prince.

During the four years from 1901 to 1905 Bernard S. Rodey was Delegate to Congress, and devoted himself to the attainment of statehood, but with the general result mentioned under Gov-

ernor Thornton's administration. Every attempt finally ended in disappointment.

HERBERT J. HAGERMAN (1906)

Early in 1906 President Roosevelt appointed Herbert J. Hagerman as governor.

Governor Hagerman was a comparatively young man, who had served as assistant secretary of legation in St. Petersburg

Four Ex-Governors on Fort Marcy Heights, July, 1912:
L. B. Prince, 1889-93.   M. A. Otero, 1897-1906.
W. T. Thornton, 1893-97.   H. J. Hagerman, 1906-07.

under Ambassador Hitchcock, since Secretary of the Interior. His father, J. J. Hagerman, was the largest property owner in the Pecos Valley, and had done very much for the development of that section.

The new governor was of liberal education and high ideals,

and had every desire to conduct a creditable administration. It was understood that he was appointed with the definite idea of reforming abuses. But his position was difficult if not dangerous, as he was naturally looked upon with distrust by the adherents of the old administration which his appointment displaced.

Friction soon arose and his enemies watched for an opportunity to dislodge the governor whom they could not control, and they finally induced the president to call for the governor's resignation. It was the almost universal sentiment, that in its manner if not in its substance, this action of the impulsive president was unjust toward his own appointee, who had incurred enmity simply by following his instructions.

During this administration the statehood question assumed new shape—that of proposed joint statehood with Arizona. President Roosevelt insisted on such jointure and finally a bill passed Congress to admit the two territories as one state, named Arizona, provided the people of each territory voted in favor of it. This idea was distasteful in both territories, which really had no interests in common. But the people of New Mexico were so anxious for self government in any form, that at the election the vote was 26,195 in favor and 14,735 against the proposition, being an apparent majority of 11, 460 for joint statehood. Probably the certainty that Arizona would defeat the measure had something to do with this result. The Arizona vote was decisively opposed to the project, which therefore failed.

George Curry (1907)

The new governor was George Curry, Rough Rider captain, official in the Philippines and personal friend of President Roosevelt, who assumed office on August 8, 1907.

Governor Curry had always been a democrat, and had held many offices in New Mexico, including that of president of the legislative council. In the Spanish War he had been a captain of a company, but unfortunately had no opportunity to see service in Cuba. Afterwards in the Philippines he was chief of police in Manila, and governor of Samar, and in all positions achieved an excellent reputation. He was an admirer of Roosevelt, and at the time in question called himself a Roosevelt republican.

As governor he showed marked ability in conciliating adverse interests, was amiable, frank and helpful, and untiring in endeavoring to make the office useful to the people. He took much interest in securing public lands for the territory, in promoting immigration, and in good roads, and was indefatigable in visiting all sections of the territory that required any attention.

The fight for statehood was vigorously pressed in Washington by Delegate Andrews. At length the so-called Hamilton Bill, prepared by the House Committee on Territories, passed the House of Representatives on Jan. 17, 1910, and went to the Senate, where a substitute prepared by Senator Beveridge was passed early in June. This was concurred in by the House on July 18, and thus the long conflict of sixty years was ended.

Finally some friction arose between the Secretary of the Interior and the Governor, and this gradually increased until the President in November, 1909, decided to make a new appointment and offered the position to William J. Mills, who for twelve years had been chief justice of New Mexico. The appointment of Governor Mills was confirmed on December 20, but in accordance with the formal resignation of Governor Curry, the change in the office did not take place till March 1, 1910. It was during this administration that the Spanish-American Normal School at El Rito was founded, in March, 1909.

WILLIAM J. MILLS (1910)

Governor Mills came to the gubernatorial office well equipped for its duties. He had legislative experience in both houses of the Connecticut legislature, and had been chief justice of New Mexico since 1898.

Much of his term of office was occupied by matters connected with the transition to statehood. On June 20, 1910, the Enabling Act was signed by the president. This was followed by the election of a constitutional convention on September 6. The convention contained 100 delegates, and consisted of 71 republicans and 29 democrats. Charles A. Spiess, of Las Vegas, was elected president. The convention met on October 3, 1910, was in session till November 21, and formulated a constitution good in most of its provisions, but not contain-

ing the new theories then called "progressive." The section as to amendments was especially objectionable on account of the difficulties that it placed in the way of constitutional changes. The constitution was very satisfactory in guarding with extreme care the rights of Spanish-speaking citizens.

The vote of the people on the adoption of the constitution was taken on January 21, 1911, when the result as recorded was 31,742 in favor and 13,399 against. There was much discussion and delay in Congress, but finally the resolution admitting New Mexico and Arizona was passed and signed by the president on August 21. The only proviso, so far as New Mexico was concerned, was that the people should vote on the proposition to facilitate the making of amendments to the constitution. As the congressional resolution provided that this question should be voted on separately, by a ballot printed on blue paper, the question was commonly called "The Blue Ballot."

The day fixed for the state election was November 7. Instantly there was much political activity throughout the state, everyone desiring to take part in this first election. With many it was the first opportunity they had ever had to vote for a governor or for a regular member of congress.

Both parties made strenuous efforts to carry the state. The republican convention met at Las Vegas on September 28, and the democratic at Santa Fé on October 2. The republicans, confident of victory, nominated H. O. Bursum of Soccoro for governor, against quite a strong sentiment. The democratic convention was less confident, and perhaps therefore more careful. It nominated William C. McDonald, of Lincoln county, for governor and placed two progressive republicans on the ticket.

The succeeding campaign was brief but vigorous, and the wide difference in the aggregate votes of the leading candidates shows that the people cast their first state ballot with care and thought. The "blue ballot" amendment received a much larger majority than any individual candidate, 34,897 to 23,831. Of the principal offices, the democrats elected the governor, lieutenant-governor, one congressman, superintendent of public instruction, secretary of state and treasurer; and the republicans the attorney general, auditor, one congressman, the commissioner of public lands and two of the three supreme judges. The total vote cast was 60,842.

Nothing now remained for the territorial government which had existed so long but to end its days with dignity and grace.

On January 6, 1912, the president signed the proclamation admitting New Mexico into the American Union.

On January 15, at noon, the first governor of the State of New Mexico took the oath of office, and the territorial authority, which had existed for over sixty years, was at an end. The ceremonies were dignified and appropriate. Governor Mills made an address, largely a review of the past; Governor McDonald took the oath, and delivered his inaugural address, which looked to the future and what it held for the welfare of New Mexico.

The flag of the nation waved from the dome of the capitol, directly over the actors in this great political drama.

The band burst into an exultant strain of patriotic music.

The New State was born. The Territory was no more.

The Past, with the finished story of almost four centuries of adventure, of trial, of achievement, closed its book.

CHAPTER XXII

Churches—Schools—Newspapers

In order to take a comprehensive view of certain subjects, it seems necessary to group together the facts connected with them rather than to scatter them in the general narrative, and this is particularly true of such distinct topics as Churches, Schools and Newspapers. With this view, therefore, the leading facts regarding these three subjects are brought together in this chapter.

CHURCHES

The introduction of Christianity into New Mexico, by the efforts of the Franciscan friars, has been referred to many times in the general historical narrative.

Thus we have heard of the friars Juan de Padilla and Luis de Escalona, and we also know the touching history of Friar Agustin Ruiz and his companions, Friars Francisco Lopez and Juan de Santa Maria.

We have read of the zeal of the Franciscans who accompanied Oñate in the colonization of the territory, and of the immediate building of the first church in New Mexico, at San Gabriel.

When Oñate went on his expedition to Quivira, in 1601, he was accompanied by Fathers Velasco and Vergara, leaving Father Escalona and four other Franciscans at San Gabriel. At this date began the complaints of the Franciscans against the injustice of the governors, which continued almost without intermission through most of the administrations under the Spanish crown.

About 1620 came Padre Geronimo de Zarate Salmeron, the most successful of missionaries, according to whom and to Benavides, 34,000 Indians were baptized and 43 churches built before 1626. In 1621 the New Mexican missions were organized as the "Custodia of the Conversion of St. Paul," in charge of the Franciscans and with Benavides himself as the first custodio.

Father Francisco de Ayeta was appointed custodio in 1674, but was absent at the time of the revolution of 1680. On August

Door of Church at Santo Domingo, 1880,
A. F. Bandelier, Standing.

10 of that year occurred the great uprising of the Pueblos, and the wholesale martyrdom of Franciscan missionaries. In a single day 21 were killed in various ways in the different pueblos where they were stationed.

CHURCHES, SCHOOLS, NEWSPAPERS. 159

The whole history of the Franciscan missions in New Mexico is one of wonderful zeal, devotion and self sacrifice. The majestic ruins of the great mission churches at Pecos, Abó, Cuará and Gran Quivira, and a host of others, bear witness to the labors of the zealous soldiers of the cross; while the existing churches in the towns of the Rio Grande valley, and at Acoma, Laguna, and other pueblos, are additional evidence of the zeal of the Christian temple-builders of those days.

During the Spanish and Mexicans eras, New Mexico was included in the Roman Catholic diocese of Durango. Episcopal visitations, however, were few and far between. Bishop Crespo came in 1725 but did not reach Santa Fé; and again in 1730 made a more extended tour.

Just one Episcopal visitation was made by Bishop Elizacochea, of Durango, in 1737, and in 1760 Bishop Tamaron made a visitation during which he is said to have confirmed 2,973 persons in El Paso, and 11,371 in New Mexico. Then for a long time New Mexico seems to have been neglected, so that Pedro Bautista Pino, when a member of the Spanish Cortes in 1812, said that he had never seen a bishop in his life until he came to Spain.

With the Mexican revolution came the withdrawal of the Franciscans and the substitution of secular priests; and these latter were largely from New Mexico itself. In numbers the clergy was greatly reduced, there being, in 1823, but five Franciscans and six secular priests in the territory. Bishop Zubiría visited New Mexico in 1833. He came again in 1837, and once more in 1850, after the American occupation.

For a long time Rev. Juan Felipe Ortiz had been vicar general in charge of New Mexico, and he was left in control by Bishop Zubiría in 1850; but the change in sovereignty caused a change in ecclesiastical relations, and the Pope erected New Mexico into a separate vicariate, with Rev. John B. Lamy as apostolic vicar. Owing to delays of travel, he did not arrive in Santa Fé until July, 1851.

In 1852 Bishop Lamy was formally given the title of Bishop of Santa Fé. He found in his new jurisdiction only ten priests. One by one their places were filled by French clergy, young men, thoroughly devoted to the bishop, the most of whom spent their lives in New Mexico in zealous parochial labors. Of the deposed Mexican clergy, two became important political factors in the territory, Padre Martinez of Taos, and Padre Gallegos

Archbishop Lamy.

of Albuquerque; the former also continued to exercise his priestly functions in a chapel at Taos until his death.

In February, 1875, Santa Fé was made an arch-diocese with Bishop Lamy as archbishop; Colorado and Arizona being within the enlarged jurisdiction.

Archbishop Lamy had all the love of horticulture characteristic of the French, and he introduced into New Mexico many improved fruits previously unknown there. The first Madeira nuts were also imported by him. He established a beautiful

Bishop's Garden, Santa Fe.

garden in the rear of the episcopal residence, having a lake with a small island in its center as one of its attractions. A photograph of this portion of the "Bishop's Garden" is here reproduced, showing it as it was kept in his lifetime.

On February 19, 1885, Bishop Salpointe, of Tucson, became co-adjutor to Archbishop Lamy, and succeeded him as archbishop on his resignation, on October 11 of that year.

In August, 1891, Rev. Placido L. Chapelle, of Washington, was consecrated as bishop and appointed as co-adjutor to Archbishop Salpointe, and on the resignation of the latter became archbishop of Santa Fé, January 9, 1894.

When he was promoted to New Orleans, Bishop Bourgade, who was one of the priests brought out by Bishop Lamy in 1869, was selected to succeed him and became archbishop January 7, 1899.

The Rev. J. B. Pitaval, of Colorado, was consecrated bishop and made assistant to Archbishop Bourgade, July 25, 1902; and succeeded the latter, after his death on January 3, 1909. All the occupants of the archi-episcopal chair of Santa Fé have been men of high character and ability, and the affairs of the Roman Catholic Church in New Mexico have been successfully conducted under their wise administration.

Down to the time of the American occupation, the Roman Catholic was the only form of Christianity known in New Mexico, and indeed there was little else until the coming of the railroad in 1879.

The first Protestant clergyman to hold services in New Mexico was Rev. Henry W. Reed, a Baptist minister, who officiated in Santa Fé in July, 1849. He erected a modest adobe church, which was dedicated January 15, 1854. In 1852 Rev. Samuel Gorman came as a missionary to the pueblo of Laguna. Years afterwards the work at that pueblo was renewed by Rev. John Menaul, a Presbyterian clergyman, who established a school and preached there for many years. He opened a printing office, in which he did the work himself, and published several pamphlets in the language of the Laguna Indians. Since the immigration from the east, the Baptists have established congregations in many places, and now have 28 churches valued at $67,300.

The Methodists were the next in the field. In December, 1850, they sent Rev. E. G. Nicholson to Santa Fé, where he conducted services for about two years, when the work was discontinued. Other attempts met a similar fate until Rev. Thomas Harwood arrived in 1871 and settled at La Junta, now called Watrous. His energy and persistence overcame all obstacles and the results are now to be seen in many missions and schools. The Methodist Episcopal church has now 51 churches in New Mexico, valued at $125,000; and the Southern Methodists, who entered the territory much later, have 25 churches with an estimated value of $70,000.

The Rev. W. T. Kephardt was the first Presbyterian missionary, and he entered upon his duties in 1851, at Santa Fé. He failed to make an impression, and soon devoted himself to editorial labors. The mission work, however, was not abandoned; in 1866 the Baptist property at Santa Fé was purchased, and after the coming of the railroad a brick church was erected in place of the old adobe structure. The Presbyterians have been very active and constant in their work, both in English and Spanish, and with schools as well as churches. They now have 44 church edifices, which are valued at over $100,000, besides their educational institutions.

The first services of the Episcopal church were held in Santa Fé in July, 1861, by the Right Rev. Joseph C. Talbot, assisted by Rev. M. A. Rich, and Rev. A. H. De Mora, the services being both in English and Spanish. In 1868, Bishop Randall, of Colorado, temporarily in charge of New Mexico, made a visitation and officiated.

In 1874 the General Convention of the Church organized New Mexico and Arizona into a missionary district and elected Rev. Wm. F. Adams, of New Orleans, as bishop. He proceeded to his new field without delay, bringing with him Rev. Henry Forrester. Bishop Adams resigned in 1877, leaving Mr. Forrester, who continued in charge in Santa Fé until the fall of 1879, when he moved to Las Vegas and built the first Episcopal church in New Mexico—a plain, adobe structure, still standing. In 1880 the district was regularly organized by holding the first convocation in Albuquerque, where Bishop Spalding, of Colorado, presided.

Soon after Rev. George K. Dunlop, of Missouri, was elected bishop, and was consecrated in November 1880. During his episcopate, stone churches were built at Santa Fé, Albuquerque, and Las Vegas, and a number of other points were occupied.

He died in March, 1888, and was succeeded by Right Rev. J. Mills Kendrick, of Ohio, who was consecrated January 18, 1889, and died in the summer of 1911. Under him the growth of the church, though not rapid, was substantial. The number of churches is 14, valued at $66,750.

The Congregationalists were prominent in New Mexico when the New West Commission was conducting the academies at Santa Fé, Las Vegas, Albuquerque, etc., and the University at Santa Fé was actively engaged in educational work. In 1881 and 1882 churches were built in Santa Fé and Albuquerque. At the present time they have four churches, valued at $20,000.

Various other Christian bodies, as well as the Jews, whose first temple was erected in 1885, are now represented in the state. All religious organizations are prosperous and doing good work.

SCHOOLS.

Although there had been some royal decrees on the subject, yet it was not until the establishment of Mexican independence that any practical movement was made toward the general education of the people; but under the new system of self-government this important subject immediately attracted attention. As early as April 27, 1822, the provincial deputation passed the following resolution: "RESOLVED, that the town councils be officially notified to complete the formation of primary public schools as soon as possible according to the circumstances of each community." Unfortunately, this had very little practical result. The sons of the wealthy in many cases were sent to Durango, St. Louis and even New York for their advanced education; but their numbers were very limited.

There were a few private schools by individual teachers, but without any organization or continuity. The best known of all of these schools was that carried on for many years in Taos by Padre Martinez. This celebrated priest was an enthusiast on the subject of education, and the result of his teaching influenced an entire generation in the north of the territory.

At nearly the same time the Rev. Agustin Fernandez had a similar school in Santa Fé. During the few years before the coming of Governor Martinez from Mexico, in 1844, there was at least a semblance of a public school, but the funds for the purpose were scanty.

Governor Martinez brought two new teachers, Edward Papy, an Englishman, and Francisco Gonzales, from Mexico, which gave quite an impetus to educational matters for a short time. But all the efforts made only led to the condition of matters described by Governor Vigil in his message to the first New Mexico legislature, in 1847. He says: "There is at present but one public school in the Territory, that located in the city of Santa Fé, and supported by funds of the county, which are insufficient to employ more than one teacher."

The first English school in Santa Fé was opened on August 28, 1848, by J. W. Dunn. In July, 1849, Rev. Henry W. Reed, a Baptist missionary, tried a similar experiment, in which Mrs. Reed assisted, and both boys and girls were received. In the fall of 1851, a Frenchman named Noel opened a school, under the patronage of Bishop Lamy. The first English school, exclusively for girls, was established in 1852 by Mrs. Howe, the wife of an army officer.

Almost at the same time, Bishop Lamy succeeded in establishing an institution for girls in the same city. After much difficulty he succeeded in inducing the Sisters of Loretto to send a sufficient number of their order to New Mexico to establish the institution. On June 27, 1852, six sisters left their home in Kentucky and proceeded on the long journey across the plains for this purpose, and four of them succeeded in arriving at Santa Fé on the 26th of September, and opened their school on New Year's Day, 1853, under the title of the Convent of Our Lady of Light, with ten boarders and three day scholars. In 1863, three sisters founded a school at Taos. A year later, they opened establishments in Mora and in Denver, and more recently went to Las Vegas in 1869, Las Cruces in 1870, Bernalillo in 1875, and other points.

In order to secure equal facilities for the boys, Bishop Lamy persuaded the Christian Brothers to come to the territory, where they opened St. Michael's college at Santa Fé in 1859, and have since extended their usefulness to Mora, Bernalillo, Las Vegas, Socorro, etc. In 1875, the Jesuits opened a college at Las Vegas, which was very successful until removed to Denver, and they have since added new fields for educational activity at Watrous, Albuquerque, etc.

The other religious bodies were not idle. In 1870, Rev. J. A. Annin, a Presbyterian clergyman, established a school at Las Vegas. This was the beginning of the Presbyterian educational work which has since become very extensive in New Mexico.

In 1871, Rev. Thomas Harwood commenced his mission school at La Junta (Watrous), and for over forty years has been the head of the Methodist educational work in New Mexico, and has seen it increase to large proportions.

In 1878, the attention of the New West Educational Commission was attracted to this territory, and on July 4, 1878, Santa Fé academy was incorporated. A year later a similar academy was organized in Las Vegas, and shortly thereafter the third was added at Albuquerque. All of these did excellent educational work which only ceased when public institutions made its continuance unnecessary. In 1881, the University of New Mexico, at Santa Fé was incorporated, to extend the work then carried on by the New West Commission, and Whitin Hall at Santa Fé was erected at a cost of $15,000 as the center of its work. The public school system was still unimportant as an educational force. The people were unaccustomed to any direct tax for such purposes, and at best their means were small.

The legislature, from time to time, passed acts intended to improve the situation, but without any actual result. Really effective measures to put a modern public school system in operation always met influential opposition.

It was not until the legislative session of 1891 that a comprehensive public school system was inaugurated. Governor Prince made that subject the salient point in his biennial message to the legislature, with a strong appeal for action. On February 12 of that year the law was passed "Establishing common schools in the Territory of New Mexico and creating the office of Superintendent of Public Instruction," which marked a new era in the educational history of the territory. During the two preceding years, three institutions of higher education had been established—the University at Albuquerque, the College of Agriculture and Mechanic Arts at Mesilla Park and the School of Mines at Socorro. All of these have constantly increased in educational character and practical usefulness as time has passed.

CHURCHES, SCHOOLS, NEWSPAPERS.

The act of 1891 provided for a territorial board of education, which included the governor and the presidents of some of the higher institutions, and for a superintendent of public instruction. From that time educational matters in New Mexico have progressed with great rapidity, the number of public schools, which was about 500 in 1891, having reached the full figure of 1,000 in 1912. The percentage of illiteracy has been rapidly reduced. Sixty thousand scholars are enrolled and 40,000 in actual attendance. The number of teachers, which was but 552 in 1891, has increased to 1,548; the great gain being in the number of women, which in the 21 years has risen from 179 to 1,043. The value of public school property is almost a million dollars; that of the state institutions over a million; of private schools about $400,000; and of the Indian schools over $400,000.

In 1891, the Goss Military Institute at Roswell became a territorial institution. The first normal school of any kind in New Mexico was held in 1891 in Las Vegas. It was continued for almost a month, from June 22 to July 17, with encouraging success; and, from this arose, almost immediately after, the establishment of two territorial normal institutions, one at Las Vegas and one at Silver City. In 1909 the Spanish-American Normal School was established at El Rito, for the important purpose of preparing native New Mexican teachers for the rural schools in the state. In recent years, the educational work has progressed very rapidly, not only in public instruction, but through a multitude of denominational and private schools in all parts of New Mexico.

Meanwhile, the education of the Indians has not been neglected. The University at Santa Fé took up this work in 1886 and established for that specific purpose the Ramona School in memory of Helen Hunt Jackson. This was successfully carried on for a number of years, until 1894, when it was superseded by the government Indian schools, established at Santa Fé and Albuquerque.

There are also local government and denominational schools for the Indians at a number of points in the state.

NEWSPAPERS

The first printing press was brought from Mexico in 1834, and the Abreu family is credited with that piece of enterprise.

One of the first specimens of printing executed in New Mexico was the proclamation of Governor Perez, greeting his fellow citizens. This is dated June 26, 1835, thirty-four days after his arrival.

The first newspaper printed in New Mexico was *El Crepusculo* (The Dawn), which was published by Padre Martinez in Taos, commencing November 29, 1835. It was the size of foolscap paper, and but four numbers were issued. Padre Martinez printed a number of small books of instruction while the press remained in Taos.

The first paper published in Santa Fé was *La Verdad*, shortly after 1840. It was the official organ, and was finally discontinued about 1843. On June 28, 1845, as a successor to *La Verdad*, appeared *El Payo de Nuevo Mejico*.

The first newspaper wholly or partly in English was the Santa Fé *Republican*, which first appeared on September 4, 1847. It was a well printed four page weekly, two pages in English and two in Spanish. The file belonging to the Historical Society begins with No. 5, October 9, 1847.

In 1849, on December 1, the *New Mexican* appeared at Santa Fé, published by Davies and Jones. The present *New Mexican* commenced publication January 22, 1863, Charles Leib being the founder. Within a year it was sold to Charles P. Clever and by him to W. H. Manderfield. In May, 1864, Mr. Manderfield formed a partnership with Thomas Tucker, and their firm continued to publish the *New Mexican* until 1880, when it was sold to a company representing the A., T. & S. F. railroad, Charles W. Greene being editor. Through a long career it has always retained a leading position in New Mexican affairs. It became a daily in 1868.

Among the early papers were:

The Mesilla *News,* issued in 1860.

The *Amigo del Pais* and the *Gaceta,* in Santa Fé, in the early "fifties."

El Democrata, at Santa Fé, by Miguel Pino, in 1859.

The New Mexico *Press,* at Albuquerque, edited by Hezekiah S. Johnson, in 1863.

The Elizabethtown *Lantern* in 1868.

With the coming of the railroad, newspapers sprang up like

CHURCHES, SCHOOLS, NEWSPAPERS. 169

mushrooms, and many perished almost as rapidly. They did good work, however, in the development of the country.

In 1850 there were but two newspapers in New Mexico; in 1870 the number had increased to five; in 1880 there were eighteen; and in 1885 there were thirty-nine papers, of which eight were dailies, a larger number of the latter than a quarter of a century later.

With the settlement of the eastern counties the number greatly increased, until, at the opening of statehood, New Mexico has no less than 125 periodicals, of which about 100 are printed in English and 25 in Spanish. Corresponding with the increasing number, has been the general improvement in size, typography, and the character of the literary work. New Mexico has no reason to fear a comparison with any of its neighbors as to the excellence of its press.

CHAPTER XXIII.

Principal Territorial Officials, 1846 to 1912.

The following list of governors includes all those who were appointed to that position while New Mexico was a territory. Under the Organic Act, the secretary became acting-governor the moment the governor left the territory. In accordance with this, every secretary acted as governor, more or less, and a full list of secretaries is therefore given.

The list of chief justices shows the heads of the judiciary through the whole territorial period.

A full list of delegates in Congress is also presented.

Governors Under Military Appointment

1846 Aug. 19, Stephen W. Kearny.
1846 Sep. 22, Charles Bent (killed Jan. 17, 1847).
1847 Jan. 17, Donaciano Vigil, acting.
1847 Dec. 17, Donaciano Vigil.
1848 Oct. 11, J. M. Washington, Commanding Department.
1849 John Munroe, Commanding Department.

Civil Governors Under the Organic Act

1851 James S. Calhoun.
1852 William Carr Lane.
1853 David Meriwether.
1857 Abraham Rencher.
1861 Henry Connelly.
1866 Robert B. Mitchell.
1869 William A. Pile.
1871 Marsh Giddings.
1875 Samuel B. Axtell.
1878 Lewis Wallace.
1881 Lionel A. Sheldon.
1885 Edmund G. Ross.
1889 L. Bradford Prince.
1893 William T. Thornton.
1897 Miguel A. Otero.
1906 Herbert J. Hagerman.
1907 George Curry.
1910 William J. Mills, till Tan. 15, 1912.

PRINCIPAL TERRITORIAL OFFICIALS.

SECRETARIES

1846 Donaciano Vigil (Appointed by General Kearny).
1848 Donaciano Vigil (Appointed by Colonel Washington).
1851 Hugh N. Smith (not confirmed).
1851 William S. Allen.
1852 John Greiner.
1853 William S. Messervy.
1854 W. W. H. Davis.
1857 A. M. Jackson.
1861 Miguel A. Otero.
1861 James H. Holmes.
1862 W. F. M. Arny.
1867 H. H. Heath.
1871 Henry Wetter.
1872 W. F. M. Arny.
1873 William G. Ritch.
1884 Samuel A. Losch.
1885 George W. Lane.
1889 B. M. Thomas.
1892 Silas Alexander.
1893 Lorion Miller.
1897 George H. Wallace.
1901 James W. Raynolds.
1907 Nathan Jaffa to 1912.

CHIEF JUSTICES

1846 Joab Houghton.
1851 Grafton Baker.
1853 J. J. Deavenport.
1858 Kirby Benedict.
1866 John P. Slough.
1868 John S. Watts.
1869 Joseph G. Palen.
1876 Henry L. Waldo.
1878 Charles McCandless.
1879 L. Bradford Prince.
1882 Samuel B. Axtell.
1885 William A. Vincent.
1885 Elisha V. Long.
1889 James O'Brien.
1893 Thomas W. Smith.
1898 William J. Mills.
1910 William H. Pope.

DELEGATES IN CONGRESS

Congress	Date	Name
31st	1849-51	William S. Messervy.
32d	1851-53	R. H. Weightman.
33d	1853-55	José Manuel Gallegos.
34th, 35th and 36th	1855-61	Miguel A. Otero.
37th	1861-63	John S. Watts.
38th	1863-65	Francisco Perea.
39th and 40th	1865-69	J. Francisco Chaves.
41st	1869-71	Charles P. Clever.

Contested by J. F. Chaves, who was finally seated.

PRINCIPAL TERRITORIAL OFFICIALS.

DELEGATES IN CONGRESS—Continued.

Congress	Date	Name
42d	1871-73	José Manuel Gallegos.
43d and 44th	1873-77	Stephen B. Elkins.
45th	1877-79	Trinidad Romero.
46th	1879-81	Mariano S. Otero.
47th	1881-83	Tranquilino Luna.
48th	1883-85	F. A. Manzanares.
49th to 53d	1885-95	Antonio Joseph.
54th	1895-97	Thomas B. Catron.
55th	1897-99	H. B. Fergusson.
56th	1899-1901	Pedro Perea.
57th and 58th	1901-05	Bernard S. Rodey.
59th to 62d	1905-12	William H. Andrews.

CHAPTER XXIV

State Organization, 1912

The state government was put in actual operation by the inauguration of the governor, on January 15, 1912. The Legislature met and organized on March 11, 1912, and continued in session until June 8. During the session of the Senate a number of the appointive officials were appointed and confirmed; a few remaining in office under their previous appointments.

The following officials were holding their respective positions on January 1, 1913.

ELECTED OFFICIALS

STATE

Governor	William C. McDonald
Lieutenant Governor	Esequiel C. de Baca
Secretary of State	Antonio Lucero
Attorney General	Frank W. Clancy
Auditor	William G. Sargent
Treasurer	Owen N. Marron
Commissioner of Public Lands	Robert P. Ervien
Supt. of Public Instruction	Alvan N. White
Corporation Commissioner	Hugh H. Williams
Corporation Commissioner	Matthew S. Groves
Corporation Commissioner	Oscar L. Owen

CONGRESSIONAL

U. S. Senators

Thomas B. Catron   Albert B. Fall

Representatives

George Curry   H. B. Fergusson

JUDICIAL

Supreme Court, Chief Justice	Clarence J. Roberts
Supreme Court	Richard H. Hanna
Supreme Court	Frank W. Parker
District Court, 1st District	Edmund C. Abbott
District Court, 2d District	Herbert F. Raynolds
District Court, 3d District	E. L. Medler
District Court, 4th District	David J. Leahy
District Court, 5th District	John T. McClure
District Court, 6th District	Colin Neblett
District Court, 7th District	Merrit C. Mechem
District Court, 8th District	Thomas D. Leib

Appointed State Officials

Traveling Auditor	Howell Earnest	1912
State Engineer	James A. French	1912
Insurance Superintendent	Jacobo Chavez	holds over
Librarian	Lola C. Armijo	holds over
Adjutant General	A. S. Brooks	1912
Superintendent of Penitentiary	John B. McManus	1912
Game and Fish Warden	Trinidad C. de Baca	1912
Captain Mounted Police	Fred Fornoff	1912

PRINCE'S STUDENT'S HISTORY OF NEW MEXICO
SUPPLEMENT, 1921

CHAPTER XXV

Nine Years of Statehood

The administration of Governor McDonald was longer than any other can be under the present Constitution. The regular term of state officers in general as provided in the Constitution then adopted, was four years, commencing on the first of January succeeding the election. To this was added the provision that "such officers except the Commissioner of Public Lands and the Superintendent of Public Instruction, shall be ineligible to succeed themseves after serving one full term." But in starting the new State government, the first term was necessarily irregular. The Constitution contained a provision that the term of office of all officers chosen at the first election should commence on the date of their qualification and expire as if they had been elected in November, 1912. They were really elected in 1911 and were sworn in on January 15, 1912, so that their terms were nearly five years instead of four; and by the same provision the two members of Congress served till March 4, 1915. By the original Constitution the terms of all county officers were fixed at four years, but no sooner had the new government organized than a strong public sentiment was developed in opposition to the length of ófficial terms, and amendments were promptly prepared and approved by the legislature and submitted to the people for adoption or rejection at the election of 1914. The subject was warmly debated in the campaign of that year with the result that the amendment reducing the term of State officers to two years was adopted by the decisive vote of 18,472 to 12,257, and the similar reduction in the term of county officers by the still stronger majority of 20,293 against 12,125. A restriction of continuous office holding in counties was secured by providing that all county officers having served two consecutive terms shall be ineligible to hold any county office for two years thereafter.

The first state election, held in November, 1911, showed that politically New Mexico was quite equally divided between the two leading parties, and also proved that the people were disposed to vote quite independently and according to their individual opinions of candidates. The Progressive Republicans made a fusion with the Democrats and received representation on the Democratic ticket, including R. H. Hanna for Supreme Court Judge. Of the principal officers the Democratic party elected the governor, lieutenant-governor, secretary of state, treasurer, superintendent of public instruction and one judge; and the Republicans secured the auditor, attorney general, commissioner of public lands, and two judges. Of the two members of Congress, one was elected by each party. The Legislature was Republican in both branches. Very rarely, if ever, have the voters of the state made such an equal division in the selection of officials. The highest Democratic vote was 31,036 for W. C. McDonald for governor, and the highest Republican vote was 30,163 for F. W. Clancy for attorney general; the six leading candidates for justice of the Supreme Court ranged between 29,423 and 29,681, a difference of less than 260 from highest to lowest. The successful candidates for Congress, Curry and Fergusson, though on opposing tickets, only varied 163 votes in a total of 60,000. The Socialist candidates received about 2,000 votes.

The result of the political division of officers and especially the fact that the first and second Legislatures were Republican, while the governor was Democratic, was to prevent anything very radical either in administration or legislation. Attempts were made to improve the system of assessment and taxation and considerable progress was made in the construction of "good roads" by united action of the National and State governments. The business of the State Land Office in the selection and administration of public land was greatly increased.

In the first legislative session public interest naturally centered largely around the election of U. S. senators. Representation in the Senate was a conspicuous feature of State government, and the senatorial selection overshadowed all other business in the Legislature until it was decided. This was fixed for

March 19, 1912, when two senators were to be chosen. The Republican majority was large, but it was agreed to hold no caucus and leave each member free to vote for any two candidates that he preferred. Long before the appointed day the capital city was crowded with politicians. The Democrats agreed to support A. A. Jones and Felix Martinez, and cast their votes accordingly throughout the contest except when complimentary votes were given for various party leaders. The Republicans were nearly equally divided among four leading candidates, A. B. Fall, William J. Mills, W. H. Andrews and T. B. Catron, with a few votes each for half a dozen others. As days passed and successive ballots were taken the excitement increased, being augmented by charges of corruption against four members of the House who were thereupon suspended. At length, on March 27, Messrs. Mills and Andrews withdrew and Messrs. Fall and Catron were elected, the final vote standing: Fall 39, Catron 38, Martinez 25, Jones 23, Prince 3, Hagerman 3, Larrazolo 2, Gillenwater 2, Romero, Mills and Sena each 1. The respective terms of the two senators were decided by lot, Catron drawing the long term and Fall the short one, but the latter was soon after elected to succeed himself. At the expiration of Senator Catron's term, in 1917, he was succeeded by A. A. Jones, and at the end of Senator Fall's second term in 1919 he again succeeded himself, but resigned in the beginning of March, 1921, in order to accept the position of Secretary of the Interior under President Harding. The vacancy thus created was filled by the appointment by Governor Mechem of Hon. H. O. Bursum on March 11, 1921.

In 1912 the people of New Mexico for the first time had an opportunity or voting for a president of the United States. Four political parties placed presidential electors in nomination, the State being entitled to three votes. The split in the Republican party following the nomination of President Taft had caused the organization of the Progressive Republican party with Colonel Roosevelt as its candidate, and that movement was then at its height and active in New Mexico. The election resulted in the choice of the Democratic electors, pledged to Woodrow Wilson for president, and the total vote, as given to the first named elector in each case, was as follows: Democratic 20,437, Republican 17,134, Progressive 8,347, Socialist 2,857.

The only official elected at this time was one representative in Congress, the apportionment bill having fixed the representation of New Mexico at one instead of the two that were hoped for. H. B. Fergusson was elected by a vote of 22,139 over Nathan Jaffa, Republican, with 17,900, Marcos C. de Baca, Progressive, with 5,883, and Andrew Eggers, Socialist, with 2,648.

At the election of 1914 the only State officials voted for were the member of Congress and one Corporation Commissioner. Benigno C. Hernandez was elected to Congress by a vote of 23,812 against H. B. Fergusson, Democrat, with 19,805, F. C. Wilson, Progressive, 1,695, and W. P. Metcalf, Socialist, 1,101. Hugh H. Williams was re-elected as Corporation Commissioner.

As the conclusion of the long administration of Governor McDonald drew near it was evident that a strong feeling existed among the citizens of Spanish parentage that the next governor should come from that element, which claimed to include more than half of the population. This feeling found expression in the Democratic State convention and secured the nomination of Lieutenant Governor Ezequiel Cabeza de Baca, who had served creditably as lieutenant governor; and Governor McDonald consented to accept the second place on the ticket in order to add to its strength. The interest in the election was largely increased by the campaign being a presidential one and also because it included the first election of a senator by popular vote under the newly adopted amendment to the United States Constitution. For this position the Democrats nominated A. A. Jones of Las Vegas and the Republicans nominated Frank A. Hubbell of Albuquerque. For governor, Mr. Bursum was again nominated, with Washington E. Lindsey of Portales as lieutenant governor.

The result, though favorable to the Democrats on the principal officers, yet was similar to the first State election in discriminating between candidates and choosing a number of Republicans. The presidential vote was 33,693 Democratic, 31,097 Republican, 1,977 Socialist, and 112 Prohibition. Jones was elected senator by 3,532 and De Baca governor by 1,823, and the Democrats also elected the congressman, secretary, treasurer, attorney general, and corporation commissioner. But the Republicans obtained a majority for Lindsey as lieutenant governor, and for auditor, superintendent of public instruction, land commissioner, and Supreme Court judge; and as events proved, the first of these offices was of special importance. When Lieutenant Governor De Baca was nominated in August his health was far from good, but it was believed that his sickness was temporary. During the campaign he struggled to take an active part, but his ill health was evident, and immediately after his election he left New Mexico for Los Angeles for lower altitude and hospital treatment, his disease being pronounced pernicious anemia. Every means was used to effect his recovery but without success, and when the time for his inauguration approached he was advised not to risk an immediate return to the altitude of Santa Fe. But he felt a conscientious obligation to perform as far as possible the duties to which he had been elected and insisted on making the journey in time for inauguration, and arrived in Santa Fe on December 30 quite exhausted, going directly from the depot to St. Vincent's Sanitarium, where he took the oath of office on New Year's Day of 1917. He was never able to leave his room, and thus never set foot within the executive office nor stepped inside the executive mansion as governor of New Mexico; but he struggled manfully to perform the most necessary duties of his position until on February 18, 1917, he peacefully passed away. He had the respect and regard as well as the sympathy of the entire community, and nothing was left undone to show the general feeling of sorrow at his untimely death. The Legislature adjourned until after his funeral, the remains lay in state at the Capitol, every official honor was rendered, and at the burial service at Las Vegas Governor Lindsey and the five living ex-governors, Prince, Otero, Hagerman, Curry and McDonald, acted as pall bearers.

Lieutenant Governor Lindsey promptly took the oath of office as governor and assumed the responsibilities of the executive office. As the Legislature was already in session and its duration was limited by law, an unusual amount of business had to be accomplished in a very short time, and the political changes in administration caused by the death of the governor added to the responsibilities of the situation.

Governor Lindsey may appropriately be called the War Governor of New Mexico. When he assumed office the great World War was practically already upon us. For considerably over a year the National Guard had been in the active service of the United States, along the Mexican border, Colonel E. C. Abbott being the chief officer in command. The raid on Columbus, in southern New Mexico, by Villa's troops, on March 9, 1916, had naturally aroused great indignation and excitement. The State troops had scarcely been relieved from duty when Congress, on April 6, 1917, declared that a state of war existed with the German Empire, and on April 21 the National Guard was again called into active service. Almost immediately Governor Lindsey issued a proclamation calling a special session of the Legislature to meet the emergency, and this convened on May 1. An excellent patriotic spirit and unanimity of sentiment brought about rapid and efficient action. The session lasted but one week, adjourning on May 8, but enacted seven laws which covered all the necessary legislation, provided for the organization of the militia, and appropriated a sum not exceeding $750,000 to be raised on certificates of indebtedness.

The war record of the State is one of honor and glory, but cannot be adequately narrated here. No part of the country responded more patriotically to the varied calls for personal service of all kinds. The official statistics show that down to October 8, 1918, 3,333 volunteers had enlisted and 8,720 drafted men had been called to the colors. They represented all kinds of nationalities and even included nearly 100 Indians. Unfortunately for State credit they were not concentrated in regiments or even in companies, but were scattered throughout the entire army, perhaps in that way being of greater service, and acting as excellent leaven for less desirable troops. They were among the first to come under fire on foreign soil, and some of them remained long after the close of hostilities in the army of occupation in the German Provinces.

It may truthfully be said that while New Mexico was the

next to the youngest State and comparatively weak in population and resources, yet in proportion to its ability no State in the Union did its part in the great war with more enthusiasm and patriotic spirit.

At the special legislative session the principal enactment was "An Act to provide for the public defense" which, in addition to the appropriation of $750,000 already referred to, created a Council of Defense consisting of nine members appointed by the governor. As the members of the Council could not all remain permanently at the capital, and its business required prompt action, an executive committee consisting of Charles Springer, B. C. Hernandez and C. R. Brice, was appointed, which continued in practical control of the varied State activities throughout the war, and is entitled to great credit for its efficiency.

In the realm of civilian activities the patriotism of the people was notably displayed. Practically the whole adult population was engaged in work of public importance, each person in the way in which he could be most useful and effective, either in organizations or as an individual. The first organized service was that of the Red Cross, which commenced as early as the spring of 1915.

In nearly every effort to raise funds the subscription exceeded the amount designated as the quota of the district interested. Thus the Y. M. C. A. campaign, which was expected to produce $30,000, really doubled its quota by raising $60,600. The Salvation Army, in 1918, instituted a general collection intended to raise $18,000, and the State responded with $24,623. The Knights of Columbus and kindred organizations did efficient and valuable work in many ways. The four great Liberty Bond campaigns present the best criterion by which to judge the spirit of service and sacrifice on the part of the people. The quotas suggested in the four cases were $1,375,400, $3,095,705, $3,658,-500, and $3,223,300, being in all $11,371,905; while the subscriptions surprised even the most sanguine prophets, being respectively $1,834,600, $3,945,750, $6,001,750, and $6,170,-

300 or in all, $17,952,400, or nearly 50 per cent above the required sum.

Apart from the semi-official organizations under the Food Administration and Fuel Administration, there were multitudes of voluntary associations and committees which rendered efficient and important services in their different spheres of activity. The number of addresses made by "four-minute men" was computed to exceed five thousand.

The women of the State showed, if possible, even a greater degree of patriotic fervor and practical service than the men. In every way their co-operation was hearty, enthusiastic and effective. Their State organization, with fourteen departments, covered the whole field of patriotic and beneficient work and laid the foundation for a comprehensive system of public welfare service which will continue long after the era of the war.

Throughout the entire administration of Governor Lindsey the war was the overshadowing interest and the governor devoted his attention to every detail of official work connected with it with an untiring energy which received general recognition. He naturally felt a desire for a continuance in office by direct election as governor in 1918, as the most practical form of expression of what seemed a general sentiment, but the party leaders believed that the political situation required the nomination of a candidate for governor representing the large Spanish element of the population and succeeded in securing the selection of Octaviano A. Larrazolo as the standard bearer of the campaign. The Democrats met this strategic move by nominating Felix Garcia of Rio Arriba County, who had the advantage of having been born in New Mexico, while Mr. Larrazolo was a native of Chihuahua. The election was warmly contested and resulted in the first decisive victory that had been obtained by either party since the establishment of Statehood, by the election of the entire Republican ticket. The average Republican vote was about 24,000 and the Democratic 23,500, with a Socialist vote of 600. The result extended Mr. Fall's senatorial position for six years, returned Mr. Hernandez to the House of Representatives, filled all of the State offices with Republicans and placed Judge H. F. Raynolds on the Supreme Bench in the place of Judge Hanna.

Mr. Larrazolo came to Santa Fe at an early age as a protegé of Archbishop Salpointe and attended San Miguel College in 1875 and 1876. He was a teacher and court clerk in El Paso for several years until his admission to the Bar in 1889 when he was almost immediately elected District Attorney. Soon after he removed to Las Vegas and took an active part in New Mexican politics, gaining many friends by his charm of manner and persuasive eloquence. He became the Democratic candidate for delegate more than once, and came within a few votes of an election. In the Statehood campaign he was an effective speaker, and when Statehood was actually secured he changed his political connections and was an influential participant in the first Republican State convention in 1911. During his term as governor his health was far from good and he was obliged to visit California and other lower altitudes, and during his absence Lieutenant Governor Pankey filled the executive chair with appreciation and popularity.

Governor Larrazolo represented New Mexico at several conferences of governors at Washington with much ability and success, and on the organization of the League of Public Land States became the foremost champion of the movement to obtain the cession by the National Government of all the public domain to the States in which it is situated and was made president of the organization. Among the notable events of this administration were the ratification by the Legislature of the Eighteenth Amendment to the Constitution (Prohibition), on January 20, 1919; and that of the Nineteenth Amendment (Woman's Suffrage), for which a special session of the Legislature was called by the governor, on February 21, 1920. By its prompt action on these important subjects, as well as by its patriotic war record and its remarkable advance in relation to education, good roads and public welfare, New Mexico has placed itself among the most progressive States in the country.

Governor Larrazolo naturally expected a renomination, but political leaders were divided in their views and the Republican State convention of 1920 was very largely attended and the scene of much excitement.

In the earlier ballots the governor showed great strength, being far in advance of any competitor and within a few votes of success, but the sudden union of all the elements opposed to his nomination finally gave a majority to Merritt C. Mechem of Socorro, who had served acceptably in the Legislature and as District Judge. On the Democratic side Judge Hanna was nominated with much enthusiasm and made a very active campaign, but the political tidal wave in favor of the Republican presidential ticket affected New Mexico as other States, and swept every Republican candidate into power.

The presidential vote was as follows: Harding 57,634; Cox 46,668, Farm Labor ticket 1,097. On governor: Mechem 54,-161, Hanna 50,535.

The State government thus became almost solidly Republican on January 1, 1921, the following persons being in office:

Governor, Merritt C. Mechem.
Lieutenant Governor, William H. Duckworth.
Secretary of State, Manuel Martinez.
Treasurer, Charles U. Strong.
Auditor, Edward L. Safford.
Attorney General, Harry S. Bowman.
Superintendent of Public Instruction, John V. Conway.
Commissioner of Public Lands, Nelson A. Field.
Corporation Commissioners: Hugh H. Williams, Jesus M. Luna, Bonifacio Montoya.
Supreme Court: Clarence J. Roberts, Herbert J. Raynolds, Frank W. Parker.

Nestor Montoya was elected representative in Congress, his term beginning March 4, 1921.

The total population of the State in 1920, by the last revised census report, is 360,350. Population in 1910, 327,301.

www.ingramcontent.com/pod-product-compliance
Lightning Source LLC
Chambersburg PA
CBHW020759160426
43192CB00006B/381